## Praise for *Investing with Impact* and Jeremy K. Balkin

"Jeremy's work is inspiring and important and speaks to the potential of a generation ready to change the world. He is a role model for young people eager to find new and innovative ways to make a difference."

—Lynn Schusterman, co-chair of the Charles and Lynn Schusterman Family Foundation

"If impact investing becomes 'business as usual,' the future will be a much different place."

—Dr. Judith Rodin, president, The Rockefeller Foundation

"Making money and doing good in the world are not mutually exclusive."

—Arianna Huffington, founder, *The Huffington Post*, and author of *Thrive*

"Leadership is much less about *how to do*, and much more about *how to be*. Jeremy Balkin's *Investing with Impact* makes a powerful case for ethical leadership in finance."

—Frances Hesselbein, CEO, The Frances Hesselbein Leadership Institute; recipient of the Presidential Medal of Freedom

"Jeremy Balkin's *Investing with Impact* is a must-read for everyone on Wall Street."

—Rina Kupferschmid-Rojas, founder & CEO, ESG Analytics AG

"Jeremy Balkin's insightful work, *Investing with Impact*, not only provides a powerful message that reshaping finance can be a powerful tool for social good, but sends a warning to the existing establishment that change is coming soon."

—Kevin Steinberg, president & Head of Client Services, Purpose

"Let's search to construct a society and an economy where man and his good, and not money, may be the center."

— Pope Francis

"*Investing with Impact* makes the robust case for market-based innovation, combined with the power of entrepreneurship and capital markets to deliver measurable positive social impact."

—The Hon. Dominic Perrottet, Minister for Finance and Services, NSW Government

"Impact investing is gathering force as more people seek to generate profit and social impact together. Jeremy Balkin's *Investing with Impact* reminds us that impact investing is ultimately a movement to reinfuse morality into markets with profound implications for how we live and work."

—Antony Bugg-Levine, coauthor of *Impact Investing* and CEO, Nonprofit Finance Fund

"*Investing with Impact* persuasively articulates how and why millennials will fundamentally transform Wall Street and corporate America."

—Joan Kuhl, international speaker and author and founder of Why Millennials Matter

"Jeremy Balkin's TEDx Talk ignited a global movement. His book *Investing with Impact* shines the light on the exciting path ahead where finance is used as a force for good."

—Shyno Mathew, co-organizer, TEDxColumbiaUniversity2015

"After all, I think that the banking system can—or should—be a force for economic development."

—Antonio Simoes, CEO, HSBC UK

"Innovation and experimentation drive our high achievers to push the boundaries of that which is possible. Jeremy Balkin thinks outside the established paradigm and outlines how *Investing with Impact* can truly be achieved."

—Professor Chris Styles, Dean, UNSW Business School

# INVESTING *with* IMPACT

# INVESTING *with* IMPACT

## *why* FINANCE *is a* FORCE *for* GOOD

JEREMY K. BALKIN

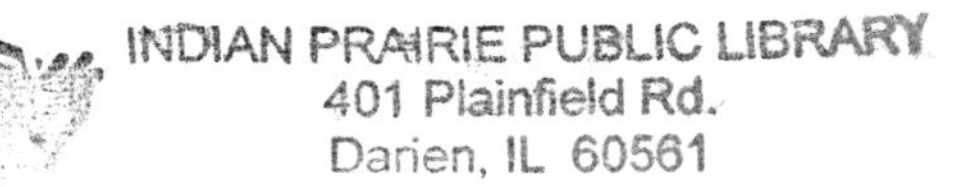

First published by Bibliomotion, Inc.
39 Harvard Street
Brookline, MA 02445
Tel: 617-934-2427
www.bibliomotion.com



Printed in the United States of America

Library of Congress Cataloging-in-Publication Data

Balkin, Jeremy K.
Investing with impact : why finance is a force for good / Jeremy K. Balkin.
pages cm
Summary: "Author Jeremy Balkin presents the case that the finance industry can improve the state of the world by positively influencing the allocation of capital"—Provided by publisher.
ISBN 978-1-62956-058-8 (hardback) — ISBN 978-1-62956-059-5 (ebook) — ISBN 978-1-62956-060-1 (enhance ebook)
1. Finance. 2. Financial services industry. 3. Investments. 4. Finance—Moral and ethical aspects. 5. Financial services industry—Moral and ethical aspects. 6. Investments—Moral and ethical aspects. I. Title.
HG173.B3343 2015
332—dc23

2015007900

*To Rebecca; Mum & Dad; and everyone who believes.*

# Contents

# Introduction

*"If we can change the culture in finance, we can change the world."*

—Jeremy K. Balkin

On September 14, 2008, I went to sleep without a care in the world, blissfully out of contact with the outside world. There was no better place to be than camping under the stars with Bedouins in the Negev Desert. I had zero ability to connect with clients, colleagues, or friends, so the world's problems would simply have to wait. The dark night sky was peaceful and eerily calm until I witnessed my first shooting star. Never the superstitious type, I didn't attach any particular significance to this event. In hindsight, though, the falling star was perhaps a symbol of what was to happen to world financial markets just a few hours later. Waking up to the sun warming the desert chill was a serenely beautiful and majestic experience—and without doubt the absolute antithesis of events taking place concurrently across the world.

Unbeknownst to me at that time, Lehman Brothers, the 158-year-old financial services firm, had filed for Chapter 11 bankruptcy protection in New York on the morning of September 15, 2008. The filing was the largest bankruptcy in U.S. history, with Lehman Brothers listing over $639 billion in assets.[1] The bankruptcy had a profound impact on the world. It began with the Dow Jones closing down over five hundred points, at the time the largest single-day point drop since the terrorist attacks of September 11, 2001. Lehman Brothers had deep exposure to commercial mortgage-backed securities, and its Chapter 11 filing setting off a sudden race to liquidate assets in a falling market. Lehman Brothers was also the prime broker for nearly one hundred global hedge funds, many of which were forced to hastily sell assets to reduce leverage, creating further market dislocation.

Money market and institutional cash funds also had significant exposure to Lehman Brothers. On September 16, 2008, the oldest money fund "broke the buck" when shares in the Reserve Primary Fund fell to 97 cents after it wrote off debt issued by Lehman Brothers.[2] There were genuine fears that a global contagion would engulf other banks, counterparties, insurance companies, asset managers, and sovereign governments. Investors were left scrambling in a financial version of musical chairs, trying to find a seat when the music of the world financial markets suddenly stopped playing. The Lehman Brothers collapse marked the beginning of a chapter in history now known as the global financial crisis.

In our modern civil society, banks are a metaphor for trust. Trust undergirds the moral fabric of the human social contract and serves as the basis for our democracy and our financial system. Thus, a banking failure sent shockwaves throughout our society's entire belief system. Former United States Federal Reserve Chairman Ben S. Bernanke filed a statement with the United States Court of Federal Claims on August 22, 2014, that read, "September and October of 2008 was the worst financial crisis in global history, including the Great Depression."[3] Bernanke continued by saying that, of the thirteen "most important financial institutions in the United States, twelve were at risk of failure within a period of a week or two."[4] Former Treasury Secretary Timothy F. Geithner is quoted in the same statement offering a similarly apocalyptic analysis. In fact, the economy was essentially in free fall in September 2008.[5] The global financial crisis had set off a chain of events almost without precedent, one that had adverse impact for people across the world.

In the years leading up to 2008, the world was enormously prosperous, with economic growth averaging above 3 percent, financial markets booming, and a very low probability of global conflict. Banking is the core constituent of the capitalist system, acting as the delivery mechanism for financial resources throughout the system. Government establishes the rules by enacting legislation that regulates the financial system and the way it operates. The question I have been trying to answer is this: Why did the economic system appear to fail so spectacularly in September 2008? The conclusion I have come to is that the economic system did not fail; nor was it allowed to fail. The free market system empowers human beings to make ethical choices between right and wrong, and the smoking gun rested in the hands of those pulling the levers at the political and financial levels. Egregious ethical failures and myopic selfishness were fuelled by excessive greed and thirst for power among those who either failed to foresee, failed to enforce, failed to regulate, or actively aided and abetted the decision making of regulators, CEOs, and bankers. In other words, human morality collectively failed. This was not simply a financial crisis, but a *morality* crisis.

## Global Morality Crisis

Morality is concerned with the distinction between right and wrong, and with discerning good and bad behavior. Ultimately, the egregious ethical decisions made at institutional levels were made by people. The profound impact of systemic institutional failure at the banking and government policy levels only demonstrates that human morality was at fault, not the system itself. The "system" ultimately is dictated, controlled, and powered by people. Hence, human morality failed because people misused the levers at their disposal, thus abusing the system. In the reckless pursuit of greed and power, there was a collective misallocation of financial resources, which led to disastrous socioeconomic consequences that will take a generation to recover from. Capitalism is an economic system that places people at the core, empowering them with the freedom to choose. In the free market system, the role of finance is to empower individuals to realize their aspirations, and in so doing lead to the betterment of society.

Leading up to the crisis of 2008, and in the years since, there were ethical failures across a wide range of industries, indicating that finance was not alone in dealing with questions of morality. However, those failures did not do the large-scale damage that the financial services sector wrought, primarily because the adverse effects of the money business are felt by almost everyone. For instance, scientists were once viewed as having high ethical standards until a string of e-mails revealed manipulation of data to exacerbate the case for global warming.[6] The media, too, have often been regarded as custodians of truth, until the phone-hacking scandal exposed blatant ethical violations at *News of the World,* a U.K. tabloid.[7] Millions of leaked diplomatic cables in 2010 further exposed ethical failings by media proprietors for withholding information important to the public. At the same time, the cables highlighted questionable government practices relating to spying on allies, as well as on methods of dealing with perceived enemies.[8]

The consequences of these ethical failures were perhaps not of the same magnitude as those in finance. In other words, nobody immediately lost his home or retirement savings because of "climate-gate" or the phone-hacking scandals, but millions of people were adversely impacted when Lehman Brothers went under. Meanwhile, finance happened to be the most visible scapegoat because a bank collapse affected everyone, whether directly or indirectly.

It was easy for people to direct anger toward a single individual; for example, Richard Fuld, the former boss of Lehman Brothers, drew public ire when it was discovered he collected $484 million in salary, bonuses, and stock options in the years leading up to the collapse.[9] People could visualize, conceptualize, and actualize their outrage toward bankers. It was easy, therefore, to make finance the symbol of profound ethical failures, and the entire industry effectively became a scapegoat for broader moral failings across society.

## A Changing World

The world is changing so rapidly that technology—and especially social media—has led us to become interdependent rather than simply interconnected.[10] There is a belief, perpetuated by governments to calm the nervous populace, that "we're all in this together."[11] Indeed, the race to the economic bottom has been neither desirable nor optimal for the 99 percent of the world's citizens who have seen their real incomes drop, watched their taxes rise, and witnessed rabid income inequality lead to a concentration of wealth in the hands of a very few while the rest increasingly struggle. As the middle class is squeezed, people compare their relative circumstances to the past rather than looking to the future. The real question—if the collapse of Lehman Brothers was the proverbial economic straw that broke the camel's back—is what do the resulting economic consequences suggest about the institutional power of the banking sector and government? On the surface, it appears that institutions are vastly more powerful than individuals, however, institutions are merely collections of citizens, who combine to form coalitions that wield power and influence. Thus, the institutions did not fail, but their leadership most certainly did. Across the world, citizens are demanding a rebalancing of economic and political power to address social dislocation and economic inequality.

Economic uncertainty since September 2008 has led to greater geopolitical instability, and the established world order remains under threat. Political processes have become hindered by multilateralism and inertia, a lack of leadership, and moral ineptitude, the results of which speak for themselves today: the United States has diminished influence in the world, making it less economically and politically secure; the European Union struggles to remain viable, with five countries requesting emergency bailouts and historically or ethnically distinct regions crying out for sovereign independence; and Russia laments the fall of the Soviet Union and exerts influence that threatens its neighbors. In Tunisia, the death of a street vendor sparked democratic uprisings across the Middle East, only to open up age-old sectarian wounds. Civil War in Syria emerged as the preferred theater of battle for the Ottomans, Persians, and Arabs to renew hostilities. China's economic progress is halted over legitimate fears about the shadow banking system and housing market, but the world focuses instead on its dispute with Japan over some obscure islands. North Korea tests its nuclear capabilities while Iran tries to acquire some for itself. Africa's economic promise is stalled by weaker export markets and an outbreak of the Ebola virus.

In the meantime, there are more than two hundred million unemployed youth[12] searching the Internet for answers. The established economic belief system is being questioned yet there is a fundamental leadership chasm, with few coherent alternatives that can restore any semblance of economic hope.

Capitalism has delivered economic growth and relative geopolitical stability for more than half a century. Simply put, economic prosperity provides people with a sense of purpose, and the lack of prosperity has created enormous problems. The collapse of Lehman Brothers may have been the straw that broke the camel's back, but the financial industry itself is not responsible for the geopolitical perils that followed. It has become evident that the lines between that which is morally right and wrong became increasingly blurred;

those who used their basic right to freedom of choice bear significant personal responsibility for their actions. In fact, the corollary to the premise that finance has played a destructive role in the modern economic landscape is that people have a limitless capacity to use the same set of resources to create a different outcome by following a different moral path. The power to effect positive change is infinitely greater in finance than it is in any other industry or sector, including government. Therefore, if we can rebalance the ethical compass and harness financial resources, we can improve the state of the world and generate positive social impact, correcting terminal mistakes of the past. That is the tipping point at which the world is currently positioned.

## Lost Decade

Seven years after the financial crisis the world has yet to fully recover, and the government response to the crisis only exacerbated the problems. My gravest fear is that the essence of the moral and ethical failures that caused the global financial crisis have been misinterpreted, misdiagnosed, and mistaken. Moreover, the pattern of unethical behavior by some of the leading financial service firms has continued, despite considerable external intervention and public outrage calling for governments to increase banking regulation. Banking scandals continue, with allegations of cartel behavior,[13] the LIBOR-rigging scandal,[14] currency manipulation,[15] gold market fixing,[16] and claims of a "boys' club" culture.[17] In spite of record fines and civil punishments, there is a lingering perception that the culture of Wall Street remains toxic.[18] In October 2014, a Rasmussen Report found that 41 percent of Americans surveyed lack confidence in the banking industry.[19] At the time of writing, more than $100 billion in fines have been imposed on banks since 2008, with more penalties likely to accrue.[20] Yet not a single banker up to this point has been personally indicted, charged, fined, jailed, or even fired for his direct involvement in the scandals leading up to and since the global financial crisis.

It appears that very little has been learned over the last seven years, and a lost decade could well become a lost century. Problems stem from the embedded culture within the industry, a culture too heavily focused on short-term personal enrichment at the expense of broader societal value creation. More than simply dictating "good" and "bad," a firm's cultural norms influence the way an employee responds to ethical questions with answers that may lie somewhere in between. In other words, culture relates to what a decision maker *should* do rather than what she *can* do, in the absence of specific regulations. It is unhelpful to attribute cultural failings to the rogue players in the industry, because culture is shaped largely at the leadership level. In fact, a broken culture is one that misprices risk, disproportionately rewards success, and fails to penalize malpractice. Perhaps some of these organizations operate beyond the scope of leadership because ethics have become *too big to scale*. In other words, as financial services firms have increased in size and complexity, the ability of senior leaders to effectively influence the collective ethical behavior of a firm is questionable because of the widening gap between employees and leadership.

Incentives—meaning, chiefly, compensation—are very strong cultural indicators, and there ought to be a shift away from rewards linked exclusively to short-term profits; these types of incentives encourage high-risk and unethical behavior. Financial service firms occupy a unique fiduciary role in the economy as the custodians of other people's money, and are therefore held to a higher standard of accountability. In fact, the financial sector performs an important public role by allocating scarce financial capital and exerting market discipline throughout the global economy. Thus, financial firms exist primarily to benefit the public, facilitating the free flow of capital throughout the financial system and generating prosperity. The finance industry must do better than it has been, in terms of transparency and public accountability, because it cannot perform its essential function without the public's trust. Cultural transformation will take shape when ethical behavior is incentivized and profit generation that achieves positive social impact is rewarded. The future belongs to those who are led by their dreams and can positively influence the allocation of capital.

## The Future Is Now

The millennial generation has been the demographic cohort most affected by the economic consequences of the global financial crisis. This generation will be 103 million strong in the United States by 2020, and it is transforming the modern ecosystem by striving for meaning and significance in an uncertain world.[21] Those of the millennial generation understand better than anyone how interdependent the world is, as they share a worldview in which common values and transparent technology empower self-belief and produce an entrepreneurial mind-set. Thus, traditional institutional authority holds less sway than moral authority. Within a decade, the millennial generation will make up the majority of eligible voters, workers, and adults in the United States, and as a result, the values of millennials will shape the future of business, government, and society. This demographic wave is unstoppable, but significantly greater economic, social, and moral damage can be perpetrated before that happens.

Millennials will not reshape capitalism; rather, they will restore it to its former glory based on a new morality. In other words, they value a set of ethical principles that leverages financial resources to do that which is right. Plato, the ancient Greek philosopher, once said, "The first and the best victory is to conquer self." Millennials see their goal as making money by doing good rather than making money by doing whatever it takes. Finance is the vehicle through which they can ensure that prosperity continues—by embracing the approach commonly referred to as impact investing, they can generate profits and positive social impact concurrently. Impact investing is becoming more common, but the finance establishment must begin to acknowledge that generating profit and positive social impact are not mutually exclusive. In order to achieve the requisite mainstream acceptance, impact investing needs to attract the vast pool of investable capital currently sitting on the sidelines.

In the United States, there are some $31.98 trillion in assets under management by pension funds.[22] Morgan Stanley estimates that $3.07 trillion in assets under management in the U.S. are broadly mandated to consider environmental, social, and governance metrics in decision making.[23] In spite of that, the World Economic Forum estimates the total size of the impact investing market to be between $25 and $40 billion.[24] Bridging the gap between investment intention and investment action is among the great moral challenges of our age. Harnessing global financial resources to achieve positive social impact can be infinitely more powerful than the status quo, with its implication that generating profit at all costs is the sole responsibility of the investment community. Impact investing is not a new investment approach; in fact, it is ages old. In my view, it best represents the essence of the capitalist system, which embraces the prosperity of one and seeks to expand it in the best interests of all. Moreover, impact investing is the investment approach that strives to generate positive social impact alongside positive financial returns and profit. Finance is about matching ideas with capital and empowering entrepreneurs, small businesses, and corporations to facilitate economic growth and human development.

This book articulates why finance is a force for good, and lays out the plan for repairing the broken world by exercising a new set of moral values in banking and financial services. It is about inspiring high school and college students to consider a career in finance. It is about encouraging disillusioned middle managers to stay in banking. It is about reengineering the industry leadership to embrace the millennial generation as their most important customer segment. Investing with impact involves simultaneously generating positive social impact and financial returns. Only business and the private sector have the capacity to raise prosperity, because government has largely run out of ideas and money after chronic economic policy failures.

The future of the world will be determined by the ethical and cultural direction of the finance industry. If we can change the culture of finance, we can mark the next century with prosperity and abundance. That is what capitalism is all about: doing well by doing good. If we step up to the plate, the problems of our time will be a mere footnote in history. Now is the time to be reminded that the free market system—with finance as its implementation mechanism—is among the greatest forces for good the world has ever seen. Together, we need to spread the message of hope as far and as wide as humanly possible, because there is simply no alternative to failure.

A better tomorrow officially starts today.

# Chapter 1

# The Blame Game

The global financial crisis of 2008 brought the world to the brink of economic catastrophe. In a March 2009 speech at the Council on Foreign Relations in Washington D.C., United States Federal Reserve Chairman Ben S. Bernanke asserted, "The world is suffering through the worst financial crisis since the 1930s, a crisis that has precipitated a sharp downturn in the global economy." Bernanke was notionally responsible for crafting the United States' monetary policy response to the global financial crisis, and his unique insight is telling. In fact, his acute understanding of the Great Depression, overlaid with the contemporary response to the global financial crisis, renders him perhaps the single greatest authority on the subject. In the same speech, Bernanke stated, "[The crisis'] fundamental causes remain in dispute," but said, "[i]n my view, however, it is impossible to understand this crisis without reference to the global imbalances in trade and capital flows that began in the latter half of the 1990s."[1]

Perhaps Bernanke is right and the global financial crisis did not happen in isolation, nor as a sudden random event. In this view, the global financial crisis was the culmination of a series of incremental events that, over time, eventually caused the economy to burst at the seams. Countless books and newspaper column inches have attempted to explain the global financial crisis; this book does not seek to add to those economic histories but rather to inspire the future direction of enlightened participants in banking and financial services. Condensing the global financial crisis into a simple television news sound bite or five-hundred-word blog post is rather difficult, and the financial system is so complex that the vast majority of people lack the necessary background to comprehend the gravity of the problem. Therefore, biases and prejudices tend to play a significant role in shaping opinions.

Clearly, there needed to be a scapegoat for the global financial crisis, so people could visualize the enemy and conceptualize an entity that could be blamed. Hence, characterizing Wall Street bankers as "evil"[2] may have appeased some because that narrative presents a simple view that banking failure alone caused the global financial crisis. However, this tendency to scapegoat created a much broader issue in the years that followed, as the concept of responsibility became a political issue, making assessments and solutions to the problems that caused the crisis more difficult to reach. In other words, if we fail to understand the proper causes of the global financial crisis, how can we correct them? The capitalist system entrusts human beings with the freedom to choose their actions, empowered by the philosophy of enlightened self-interest. In 2008, the system itself did not fail; rather, the crisis represented a collective moral failure of the participants in the system. Assigning blame to individuals or firms is neither accurate nor effective as a means of understanding the failure.

In February 2009, *Time* magazine produced a list of "25 People to Blame for the Financial Crisis."[3] Interestingly, number three on the list is the immediate predecessor of Ben Bernanke, former United States Federal Reserve Chairman Alan Greenspan. Described as "an economist and a disciple of libertarian icon Ayn Rand," Greenspan "presided over a long economic and financial-market boom" and "attained the status of Washington's resident wizard." *Time* added, "his long-standing disdain for regulation" would be one of the "leading causes" of the mortgage crisis. This analysis may reflect Greenspan's personal preference for laissez-faire regulation, but ultimately the responsibility of making and enforcing laws resides with the government, not the central bank. Therefore, laying blame for the global financial crisis on any single individual, let alone on an eighty-three-year-old man, seems as ethically flawed as some of the broader moral failures permeating society in the lead-up to the crisis.

*Rolling Stone* magazine offered an alternative analysis regarding "the history of the recent financial crisis" in a July 2009 article. Whereas *Time* compiled a list of people responsible, *Rolling Stone* argued, "The world's most powerful investment bank is a great vampire squid wrapped around the face of humanity, relentlessly jamming its blood funnel into anything that smells like money."[4] Perhaps unbeknownst to many, Goldman Sachs was "the world's most powerful investment bank," apparently, given the coincidence that numerous former employees occupied key roles within the United States Treasury and rival firms at the time of the collapse of Lehman Brothers. The article failed to clearly articulate what motivation, if any, former Goldman Sachs employees would have to give preference to their former firm at the time of the global financial crisis. In fact, it is ridiculous to lay blame on firms like Goldman Sachs that remained robust during the crisis rather than attributing any responsibility to the firms like the shadow banking clique, including Lehman Brothers, that monumentally collapsed, resulting in the chaos of the global financial crisis.[5] Conspiracy theories may be attractive and commercially lucrative on the newsstand, but they fail to address reality.

As elements of the media fuelled the blame game, the witch hunt and outcry for mob justice continued unabated. Unsurprisingly, the global financial crisis brought an increase in age-old conspiracy theories and rhetoric targeting minority groups. In a report published by the Anti-Defamation League in 2008, National Director Abraham H. Foxman explained, "Hate groups and anti-Semites used the global economic downturn to breathe new life into old myths of greedy and money-hungry American Jews, and these took on a life of their own on the Internet and in the real world."[6] In a study published in June 2009 by the *Boston Review*, titled *State of the Nation: Anti-Semitism and the Economic Crisis*, a strikingly high 38.4 percent of people surveyed attributed at least some level of blame for the crisis to Jews.[7] The historical inaccuracy of attributing blame to members of the Jewish faith, who make up less than 0.2 percent[8] of the world population and just 2 percent[9] of the U.S. population, provided an intriguing explanation as to the cause of the global financial crisis. Nonetheless, the results are deeply concerning for a country that prides itself on diversity.

Diversity of opinion and freedom of speech are hallmarks of the vibrant democracy of the United States, and are enshrined in the Constitution. The ultimate arbiter of a robust democracy, however, is the degree to which people can criticize their elected officials. In 2012, the Pew Research Center conducted a study about where middle-class Americans place "blame" for their financial woes and found that 62 percent blamed Congress "a lot."[10] After all, it was Savoyard philosopher Joseph-Marie de Maistre who wrote in 1811, "Every nation gets the government it deserves."[11] Unsurprisingly, when the respondents were asked whether they blame themselves, nearly half, 47 percent, replied "not at all."[12]

There is a unique connection behind the respective possible causes, be they plausible or implausible, of the global financial crisis. Put simply, humans are responsible for the failures that led to the economic devastation that began in September 2008 with the collapse of Lehman Brothers. Humans were entrusted with the freedom to exercise choice in their decision making, empowered by the moral philosophy of enlightened self-interest. Therefore, virtually all human beings ought to collectively share at least some element of responsibility for the egregious moral and ethical failures that were propagated at the time of the crisis. After all, as a society we benefited directly or indirectly from the increased employment, rising stock market, booming housing market, higher government tax revenues, and increased economic activity propagated at the time. It is therefore disingenuous to accept the rewards without accepting at least some degree of the responsibility.

There is no doubt that some sections of the population are disproportionately more responsible for sowing the seeds for the global financial crisis than others, including excessively greedy Wall Street bankers and traders. In October 2014, former chairman of the Swiss National Bank, Philipp Hildebrand, told a panel at a meeting of the International Monetary Fund that "this was not just a problem of rogue individuals."[13] Mr. Hildebrand went a step further and explained that "very significant sectors of society were in on this. We all have to recognize this was not just the failure of individuals, but a collective failure of society at large."[14] Indeed, leading figures in other sections of the community, including politicians, were eager to be associated with the wealth and excesses of prominent financial figures in the lead-up to the 2008 crisis, and were beneficiaries of the boom times. Ultimately, we cannot change the past, but we all share responsibility for the outcomes perpetrated by the moral and ethical failings and have a vested interest in repairing the broken world for future generations. If we fail to address these core issues, there will be change imposed by outside interests in ways that are counterproductive to future growth and prosperity.

## You Break It, You Own It

Article I, Section 1, of the United States Constitution reads, "All legislative Powers herein granted shall be vested in a Congress of the United States, which shall consist of a Senate and House of

Representatives."[15] Members of Congress are elected by the citizens of the United States and bear responsibility for regulatory oversight failure. In 2011, the 108th mayor of New York City, Mayor Michael R. Bloomberg, said, "It was not the banks that created the mortgage crisis. It was, plain and simple, Congress who forced everybody to go and give mortgages to people who were on the cusp."[16] Mayor Bloomberg's comment is particularly insightful given his immense experience in financial services and politics, and offers a unique perspective on the root causes of the crisis.

Clearly, the U.S. government played a significant role in the lead-up to and aftermath of the global financial crisis. In a democracy, elected officials enact legislation and regulations that establish the rules of the game. Government enacted legislation that actively facilitated the rapid expansion of financial institutions. Specifically, the Gramm-Leach-Bliley Act was passed in 1999 and effectively repealed part of the Glass-Steagall Act of 1933, which had prohibited any one financial institution from acting as any combination of a commercial bank, investment bank, security firm, or insurance brokerage. Repeal of Glass-Steagall and replacement of it with the Financial Services Modernization Act (Gramm-Leach-Bliley) became law under the forty-second president of the United States, Bill Clinton. This single legislative measure, signed into law by the rhythmical stroke of the president's pen, would herald a brave new world of global banking growth, merger and acquisition, and consolidation.

The government benefited greatly from the increased economic activity and tax revenues created by the economic boom. The financial services industry made up 10 percent of total U.S. corporate profits in 1949, peaked at 40 percent in 2003, and was over 30 percent in 2014.[17] Decades of *financialization,*[18] a term economists use to describe the growing size, deregulation, scale, and profitability of the financial sector relative to the broader economy, allowed banks to grow massively in the years leading up to the global financial crisis. By 2006, the financial services industry contributed 8.3 percent to U.S. gross domestic product, compared with 4.9 percent in 1980 and 2.8 percent in 1950.[19]

As economic globalization expanded in the 1990s, financial services industry modernization was required to keep pace with the growth. This required further deregulation, with reductions in bank lending and leverage restrictions effectively removing the impediments to continued global economic growth. In 2004, the U.S. Securities and Exchange Commission amended the net capital rule and permitted broker-dealers with at least $5 billion in "tentative net capital" to apply for an exemption from the established calculation method for computing net capital. The "Bear Stearns exemption"[20] effectively replaced the 1977 net capitalization rule that capped a twelve-to-one leverage limit, allowing banks to increase leverage unchecked. Bear Stearns would eventually collapse, in March 2008, with leverage as high as $42 of debt for every $1 in equity.[21]

More debt allowed banks to have more money to play with. Excessive leverage was allowed because the cost of debt was so cheap, fuelled by record-low interest rates. As globalization spread capitalism across the world, banks played a critical role in the facilitation and disbursement of financial capital internationally. In this brave new world of financial innovation and banking economies of scale, the circumstances essentially created a Pareto efficient outcome, in which customers, shareholders, and governments all benefited. "Pareto efficiency" refers to a situation in which resources are distributed in such a manner that one stakeholder cannot benefit without making another stakeholder's situation worse. It is important to remember that massive global banking expansion was not driven solely by the invisible hand of the market, altruism, or even the customer's best interest. In delicate yet simple terms, bigger banks meant bigger profits. Bigger profits meant bigger executive bonuses. Bigger bonuses also created an incentive to take bigger risks. These risks eventually became so big that certain banks were deemed *too big to fail.*

## Biting the Hand That Feeds

In testimony on June 6, 2009, in front of Congress, United States Treasury Secretary Timothy Geithner stated, "I think that although many things caused this crisis, what happened to compensation and the incentives in creative risk taking did contribute in some institutions to the vulnerability that we saw in this financial crisis."[22] On balance, Wall Street's compensation structure was skewed toward short-term performance, giving traders huge incentives on the upside and very low risk to themselves on the downside. In a system where some financial institutions are deemed too big to fail, the economic risk is mispriced and effectively transferred from the private sector to the government backstop. Essentially, the financial gains are generated by the private banking sector but losses are incurred by the government, or, specifically, the taxpayer. In other words, Wall Street is bailed out by Main Street.

Critics of "too big to fail" like former head of the United States Federal Reserve Alan Greenspan argue that, "If they're too big to fail, they're too big,"[23] and therefore believe that such large organizations should be deliberately broken up if their risk management is ineffective. These critics argue that the problem of moral hazard arises, whereby there exists an incentive to seek private profit from protective public policies. This comes about when certain firms deliberately take excessively risky but high-return positions based on the preferential public policy settings that systemically important financial insitutions received. Wall Street compensation structures played a role in encouraging risk taking and provided perverse incentives and disproportionate rewards for profits generated by unethical behavior.

However, it is disingenuous to simply apportion blame to Wall

Street in isolation. Players in the financial services industry were manufacturing and selling products that other firms, investors, and institutions were actively buying. In effect, supply was meeting investor demand. After all, investors—including pension funds responsible for managing assets for millions of Americans—were large customers for these mortgage-backed-debt investment products. Pension fund holders, while not directly employed in financial services, benefited too, gaining higher returns on traditionally low-risk investment options. Many of these pension fund holders were also benefiting from borrowing the same cheap money to buy the same overvalued homes, all as a result of record-low interest rates, which distorted asset prices. Millions of people across America were buying houses and putting money into the booming stock market, and were seeing an increase in their personal wealth as a result. Government received enormous tax revenues from income, capital gains, and corporate profits.

When the music was playing, all parties thought they had a seat—until the game of musical chairs was exposed. As the regulators, the government apparently failed to foresee the crisis and to act effectively before it got wildly out of control. Perhaps the sixteenth president of the United States, Abraham Lincoln, said it best in the Gettysburg Address: "Government of the people, by the people, for the people," underscoring the symbiotic relationship of people and their government in a democracy.[24] As they say, "no conflict, no interest,"[25] and the financial merry-go-round continued, with vast segments of the economy having some direct or indirect involvement in the party. It seems misguided to isolate the problem to just a few "greedy bankers"[26] when there were multiple mouths being fed by the same financial services–created magic pudding.

## Moral Courage Determines the Culture

Moving forward there must be a values realignment to ensure that the moral and ethical failures that led to the global financial crisis are unable to return and again cause such carnage. Values create the culture in any society or organization. Culture therefore shapes behavior, and that is heavily influenced by incentives. Ambition and hunger are important attributes we want in our financiers, but not at the expense of a philosophical understanding of the raison d'être of financial services. Ultimately, it is behavior that leads to action. If the actions are negative or perceived to be wrong, then it is important to identify where the process requires repair.

Indeed, a fundamental change in the culture of banking is still needed, with a greater focus on long-term profitability and investments that intentionally create a positive impact on society. Since the global financial crisis began in 2008, the legal tab for credit-crisis and mortgage-related settlements at the six largest American banks is more than $107 billion and is likely to increase in the coming years.[27] The *Wall Street Journal* wrote in October 2014 that, "Bankers need to undergo an ethical transformation in order to ensure the financial system is no longer a threat to prosperity and trust in free markets."[28]

That being said, rules governing personal culpability and compensation levels will not guarantee ethical behavior. During a recent International Monetary Fund meeting, Bank of England Governor Mark Carney said, "We can align compensation, we can in legal terms enforce greater personal responsibility, but ultimately it's about the individual seeing their broader responsibility for their clients and their society."[29] Incentives are therefore a critical lever that can be used to excommunicate rogue elements and to reward honest players. While incentives are largely determined from within, outside investors have a major role to play in realigning the direction of the entire financial services industry. Investing with impact has the power to change the way the entire financial services industry operates by actively rewarding companies that deliver measurable positive social impact and profitability.

The culture in financial services has a tendency to reward entrepreneurial thinking and creative endeavor in the short run. There is a fine line between the way a banker *should* behave and the way a banker *can* behave. In our highly litigious and rules-based world, the lines are often blurred between what a person should do as opposed to what she can do legally. Every person on the planet has a role to play in promoting freedom and prosperity. It is no longer sufficient to hide behind a system in which actions are dictated by endless rules governing a minority that stifle the human freedom of the majority. After all, the rules of the game need to be effective and enforceable, but the players also need to accept responsibility for their actions. It is not acceptable to rely on an antiquated political and legal system that was enacted hundreds of years ago and that does not necessarily reflect the hyperconnected, technology-driven world in which we all live. Financial services has always been, and always will be, a highly regulated industry. Dealing with money, and especially other people's money, requires a heightened fiduciary responsibility and a level of trust. Yet, despite massive regulations across the finance industry, fraudulent activity and unethical practices continue to occur. The sanctions are questionable, if not nonexistent, and the penalties are often exacted using shareholder money.[30] In fact, the risks are shared but gains are privatized. This is not how capitalism and free markets were intended to operate, and the culture that permeates financial services is clearly not sustainable.

The free market system means that every person has a stake in the outcome, because each person is able to exercise personal enlightened self-interest. That is, people who serve the best interests of society ultimately act in their own self-interest. We need to empower people in finance to demonstrate moral courage when embracing their inherent right of freedom to choose, encouraging them to act in a moral and ethical fashion that is beneficial to all participants in the marketplace and not just a select few.

## Questioning the Belief System

The global financial crisis left an indelible mark on the world, as it brought up questions about capitalism as the preeminent economic system. The leader of the Catholic Church, Pope Francis, claimed the economic flaws had stemmed from humankind's obsession with money. In a *Daily Mail* article published in June 2014, Pope Francis remarked, "At the centre of all economic systems must be man, man and woman, and everything else must be in service of this man."[31] The pope went a step further, stating, "But we have put money at the centre, the god of money. We have fallen into a sin of idolatry, the idolatry of money." However, it is clear that the pope's reference to money at the center of the system indicates that a perversion of capitalism has developed. This deviation from capitalism as it was originally intended—as a moral philosophy that empowers human beings by embracing enlightened self-interest—has resulted in the terrible economic imbalances we see in the world today.

The global financial crisis demonstrated a fundamental deviation from the essence of capitalism, characterized by egregious human misrepresentation of enlightened self-interest, collective moral failure, and ethical violations. Capitalism itself did not fail, because failure rests with the unenlightened human beings participating in the system who acted with myopic selfishness.

This broken world does not need inclusive capitalism,[32] conscious capitalism,[33] crony capitalism,[34] or even capitalism 2.0,[35] because capitalism does not need to be repaired. It is human morality that needs repairing; the world can no longer afford to flirt with an alternative system that stifles prosperity and human development.

At this point in history, continued human development depends on the restoration of human beings to the core of the economic system, because people have never before been more connected with and dependent upon one another. Capitalism has more than 4.5 billion[36] disciples scattered throughout the world, and billions more yearn for the same freedom, aspirational opportunity, and economic prosperity. Apportioning blame for the crisis serves little purpose in the pursuit of rebuilding the economy. It is the freedom of the capitalist system that allowed market participants to engage in the morally and ethically challenged behavior that led to the global financial crisis. Therefore, rather than looking to the past, we ought to pursue the essence of capitalism, which is powered by impact investing and positive social impact.

# Chapter 2

# Consequences of the Crisis

According to the World Bank, in 2013 the United States accounted for 22.4 percent of world gross domestic product.[1] As the world's largest economy, the U.S. has a profound impact on the global economy as a whole. According to the International Monetary Fund, growth in the U.S. economy was 2.7 percent in 2006 and 5.1 percent for the world economy. However, by 2013 the world economy had contracted to 2.9 percent growth as the economic growth in the United States slowed to 1.9 percent.[2] The International Monetary Fund also cut global growth forecasts for 2014 and 2015, warning that the world economy may never return to the pace of expansion seen before the crisis.[3]

Indeed, the global financial crisis was the culmination of moral and ethical failures across society, an egregious violation of the ethical philosophy of enlightened self-interest, which holds that people who act to further the interests of others ultimately serve their own self-interest. The antithesis, myopic selfishness, or *unenlightened* self-interest, results when people are excessively greedy and the interests of others suffer loss because of conflict and decreased efficiency. Myopic selfishness can result in the *tragedy of the commons,*[4] an economic theory according to which individuals acting rationally and independently according to each one's self-interest behave contrary to the whole group's long-term best interests by depleting some common resource. There is little doubt that excessive greed and myopic selfishness were rampant in the lead-up to the global financial crisis, and culminated in the worst economic circumstances since the Great Depression. The crisis was a failure made by humans, and it bequeathed a shameful economic legacy for future generations.

According to the Census Bureau, the United States is endowed with some 126 million people aged thirty years or younger, equivalent to 40 percent of the population. This contrasts distinctly with the heavily aging populations of the major global economic rivals to the United States, specifically China, Japan, and the European Union. There are significant economic benefits for countries that have predominantly younger populations in the prime of their wealth-generating capacity. Likewise, there are substantial economic constraints for nations with predominantly older populations with less economic growth capacity. In the lead-up to the global financial crisis, most of those under thirty years of age were too young to benefit directly from the financial boom times. They were simply too young to buy homes with easily available credit, build robust stock portfolios, or earn multimillion-dollar bonuses.

While the United States is blessed with an abundance of ambitious young people, they are supremely burdened by a weak economy that suppresses their opportunities. The profound words of Abraham Lincoln still hold true: "You cannot escape the responsibility of tomorrow by evading it today."[5] Younger Americans have arguably paid the dearest price in terms of lower real wages, higher unemployment and underemployment, and higher taxes. Therefore, it is essential to economically empower the next generation, as they will drive the U.S. and the world economies over the coming decades.

## Millennials

The baby boomers are documented as the wealthiest generation to date. Historically, those of each successive generation has proven wealthier than their forebears, and they hope their prosperity paves the way for their children. Offspring of baby boomers and generation Xers, those born between 1980 and 2000, are affectionately described as the millennial generation, or simply *millennials*. Unfortunately, the Center for American Progress[6] reports that millennials, on the whole, will not match or supersede the prosperity of their parents.

According to the United States Census Bureau, in July 2013 millennials aged eighteen to thirty-four accounted for 23.5 percent of the population, approximately 74.3 million people. Compare this with baby boomers aged fifty to sixty-four, who accounted for 19.6 percent of the population, or 61.9 million people.[7] As demographic trends evolve, the relative needs of each generation change with time. It is no surprise, therefore, that the propensity of older citizens to live off savings and work less is offset by the tendency of younger citizens in the wealth-accumulation phase to work more. If older Americans are working less and require greater financial assistance, while younger Americans are under- or unemployed, the ability to fund these entitlements is limited and can stunt future economic growth. The needs of America's aging baby boomers, in combination with the limited earning capacity of millennials, threaten to bankrupt the nation, which spent $773 billion, or 22 percent of its federal budget, on Social Security in fiscal year 2013.[8] It is equally concerning for the 61.9 million baby boomers in America that 74.3 million millennials are being economically stifled by record public debt, which younger generations will inherit. While this is a huge problem for the country, it is potentially calamitous for the millennials, who face the prospect of sharply higher taxes to pay for entitlement programs with little chance of ever being the beneficiaries. The challenge, therefore, arises with the sacrifices each generation makes for each other and with the economic benefits millennials are prepared to sacrifice for their forebears.

The corollary to that equation is a working-age population that has reduced capacity to generate enough tax revenue to fund the needs of the elderly, who are more reliant on government assistance. At the same time the elderly population in the United States is rising, the number of workers who pay into Social Security relative to the number who paid in in the past is decreasing. According the book *The Coming Generational Storm,*[9] by 2030 there will be about two workers per retiree, down from 3.4 workers in 2000. As a result, lower disposable incomes means millennials will be unable to allocate capital to productive income or to the growth-producing assets required to grow the nation's asset base. This will impede economic growth and the younger generation's ability to generate wealth, potentially triggering a lower standard of living for all. These factors are independent of the economic perils that resulted from the global financial crisis, indicating the enormity of the generational economic challenge.

The global financial crisis shook to the core the foundations of the economic and political system. The government policy response to the crisis led to adverse economic and social outcomes for millennials, and for the first time in their lives, millennials' beliefs in the system were challenged. According to a study by the Pew Research Center, in 2014 exactly half of millennials describe themselves as political independents and 29 percent say they are not affiliated with any religion.[10] Compared to data compiled by Pew Research Center over the past quarter century, these figures are at or near record levels of religious and political disaffiliation. The global financial crisis led young people to fundamentally question the philosophical basis for trust in traditional institutional authority.

According to the Pew Research Center, millennials are the most skeptical of citizens. In terms of social trust, just 19 percent of millennials say most people can be trusted, compared with 40 percent of baby boomers.[11] These results are entirely consistent with the premise that banking is a metaphor for trust; banking failures in 2008 left an indelible mark on millennials' sense of trust. The egregious moral and ethical failures that caused the global financial crisis understandably led millennials to respond with tremendous distrust and skepticism toward established political and economic leadership.

In 2014, the collective buying power of U.S. millennials was $1.3 trillion,[12] equivalent to 8 percent of the United States' gross domestic product. By 2020, millennials will make up 40 percent[13] of eligible voters and 75 percent[14] of the adult workforce. French philosopher Auguste Comte is credited with the statement that "demography is destiny," and demographic trends are such that millennials are rapidly coming of age, both politically and economically. Therefore, millennials have the capacity to unleash a tidal wave of monumental significance, dictating the political and economic policy direction of the United States and fundamentally reshaping the future of prosperity across the world.

## Intergenerational Economic Warfare

In March 2013, the *New York Times* asked, "Do Millennials Stand a Chance in the Real World?"[15] The article laid out the rather depressing economic reality for young people in the United States. It concluded by stating, "Millennials are the best-educated generation ever. Their challenge may just be to preserve that advantage for their own children."[16] As a generation, millennials were economically destroyed by a crisis they contributed very little to. Yet the economic consequences of the global financial crisis have been tattooed on millennials, acting as a stark reminder of the profound moral and ethical failure of the generations before them.

There is the real prospect of intergenerational conflict for the first time in the United States' history, according to Paul Taylor, author of *The Next America: Boomers, Millennials, and the Looming Generational Showdown*.[17] In other words, the more affluent baby boomers, who were the beneficiaries of the "greatest welfare program in American history," are "bankrupting" the younger generations.[18] There will indeed need to be a very delicate political and economic balance between honoring the obligations to baby boomers and avoiding bankrupting millennials. According to the Pew Research Center, 51 percent of millennials do not believe there will be any money for them in the Social Security system by the time they retire, while 39 percent think the system will only be able to provide retirement benefits lower than those of current retirees. A mere 6 percent of millennials expect to receive Social Security benefits at the same levels enjoyed by current retirees.[19]

There is a deeply concerning chasm between the needs and wants of each generation, as 53 percent of millennials believe the government should give higher priority to programs that benefit themselves, millennials specifically. This compares to just 28 percent of baby boomers who agree millennials should be preferenced.[20] This generational gap in economic perspectives is deeply concerning due to the moral hazard of current policymakers, who belong predominantly to the baby boomer generation. It is the current crop of baby boomer policymakers who will directly benefit from policies that favor their demographic cohort. If circumstances continue to deteriorate, there is also the potential for intergenerational economic warfare in the future. Therefore, a delicate balance will need to be struck between conflicting generational priorities, given the looming majority constituency of millennials.

## Lost Generation

In March 2014, an article in the *Atlantic* claimed, "This generation is getting totally screwed by the economy."[21] The rationale is that millions are graduating with a college education with virtually no savings, record student loans, and dim employment prospects due to the economic consequences of the global financial crisis. The article outlined that unemployment among younger millennials is 13.5 percent, and 12 percent for older millennials, according to the United States Bureau of Labor Statistics.[22] According to the *Wall Street Journal*, almost 300,000 Americans with college degrees were working in minimum wage jobs, approximately 70 percent more than a decade prior. In the college graduating class of 2010, nearly 50 percent are working in jobs that don't require a college degree.[23] Furthermore, approximately 37 percent of Americans between the ages of eighteen and twenty-nine have been either unemployed or underemployed at some point during the recession, according to the Pew Research Center.[24]

Perhaps more concerning are the global economic consequences for millennials as a result of the global financial crisis. In February 2014, the *Elite Daily* published an article titled "The Second Lost Generation: Why So Many Millennials Are Failing to Launch."[25] The article highlighted a variety of troubling social trends, but the most disconcerting conclusions drawn were on the economic front. "Nearly 80 percent of those surveyed are in debt, be it from student loans, credit cards, or mortgages."[26] These factors are stifling any real prospects of economic empowerment for the generational cohort that accounts for almost one in four Americans.

"The Lost Generation" is a term used to describe the generation of young people who came of age during World War I. Popularized by Ernest Hemingway, the phrase was first used by Gertrude Stein's garage owner, who noted the confusion and directionless quality of those who'd survived the war. In the context of millennials, the Lost Generation analogy has been applied to reflect their dismal economic prospects. Since the start of the global financial crisis, a quarter of millennials have endured extended unemployment for six months or more.[27]

According to a report by the International Labour Organization, in 2012 youth unemployment was close to seventy-five million young people worldwide. In addition, more than two hundred million young people are working but earning less than $2 per day.[28] It is important to note that the World Bank defines extreme poverty as an income in the developing world of $1.25 or less per day.[29] There is little doubt that youth unemployment is a monumental global challenge, yet investing in youth is akin to investing in the future engine of a prosperous society. The International Labour Organization report acknowledges that young people "represent the promise of changing societies for the better," but continues to outline the real and present danger of the "youth employment crisis."[30] Unemployment and underemployment both carry very high social and economic costs and threaten the fabric of civil society. The report highlights that failure to generate sufficient jobs can result in long-lasting "scarring" effects on young people. Therefore, the need to reverse the trend is urgent.[31]

In June 2014, Pope Francis, leader of the Roman Catholic Church, launched a scathing attack on the "atrocity" of youth unemployment in an interview with Spanish newspaper *La Vanguardia*.[32] The pope's assertion that "Our global economic system can't take any more" has effectively raised the issue of youth dislocation from an economic issue to a moral one. It is tacit acknowledgment that the systemic economic policy failures that occurred in the lead-up to and the aftermath of the global financial crisis must be addressed by a new philosophical approach that will rebuild the world's economic fortunes. Pope Francis went a step further and claimed, "We discard a whole generation to maintain an economic system that no longer endures," and warns that the high levels of youth unemployment will lead to a "lost generation."[33] For the first time in modern history, a major religious figure has entered the general political debate and articulated an economic position that has broad-ranging denominational appeal. Representing 1.23 billion people, or 17 percent of the world's population, Pope Francis recognized the pervasive links between depressed economic conditions and higher poverty rates,[34] as well as to reduced employment prospects, decreased marriage rates, and increased family breakdown. This unprecedented papal intervention has brought attention to the adverse economic circumstances facing young people around the world, appropriately characterizing the situation as a moral issue rather than purely an economic issue.

Record youth unemployment has also burdened millennials in ways that are perhaps less well understood by economists. In March 2012, the *New York Times* published "The Go-Nowhere Generation," arguing that the weak economy has increased risk aversion and led millennials to become "Generation Why Bother."[35] The economic consequences of the global financial crisis burdened millennials with higher unemployment, greater personal and student debt, and a distrust of leadership. Millennials are also delaying marriage: according to the Pew Research Center, in 2014 just 26 percent of millennials are married, compared with 48 percent of baby boomers who were married at the same age. Interestingly, 69 percent of millennials say they "would like" to marry but lack the perceived marriage prerequisite of a solid economic foundation, demonstrating the significance of adverse economic circumstances.[36] These figures are concerning for a variety of economic and moral reasons: for thousands of years, an important constant in human society has been the foundation built around family.

The Heritage Foundation published a paper in 2010 titled, *Marriage: America's Greatest Weapon Against Child Poverty*. The research highlighted that child poverty is an ongoing national concern with major economic ramifications. It should be noted that in 2010, 60 percent of children born in the United States were born to married parents, compared with 93 percent in 1960.[37] According to the United States Census, in 2008 the poverty rate for single parents was 36.5 percent; compare that to the poverty rate for married couples with children, at 6.4 percent.[38] Therefore, the Heritage Foundation argued, being raised by a married couple reduced a child's probability of living in poverty by 82 percent.[39] Recognizing this pattern, the *New York Times* published an article in February 2014 titled, "Can Marriage Cure Poverty?"[40] The self-fulfilling prophecy of higher unemployment and depressed economic conditions offers little promise or, indeed, hope to the least affluent in society to break free of their economic circumstances and undertake "family planning in the name of upward mobility," according to the article.

It is therefore unsurprising that a Pew Research Center survey in 2014 found that, spanning all generations, about seven in ten Americans say that millennials face more economic challenges than their elders did when they were first starting out.[41] This perception, backed by the economic reality, is deeply alarming for the future prosperity of the United States as a whole.

Despite the depressing outlook, millennials are far more optimistic about their economic future than any other generation. In fact, millennials have been described as "stubborn economic optimists" by the Pew Research Center report, with 85 percent saying they either currently have enough or expect to in the future.[42] No doubt some of this optimism simply reflects the timeless confidence of youth.

The broader implication is that millennials have opted to pursue a different economic approach from the one baby boomers pursued, as they painfully learned the failed lessons of the past. In so doing, millennials are following an alternate path to restoring long-term economic prosperity by embracing the very best of the ethical philosophy of enlightened self-interest and free markets, inspired by the dynamism of their entrepreneurial peers and utilizing the latest technology to solve social and economic problems simultaneously.

## Crony Capitalism

Millennials have grown up in an era of big government, with heightened security requirements limiting personal freedoms. In spite of numerous policy failures and their economic consequences, millennials accept that government has a role to play in their lives. The question is, how big a role? The economic outcomes of the last two decades of government interventionist policies in the United States speak for themselves. In 2014, federal government debt is fast approaching $18 trillion. The poor economy is having a crushing impact on millennials, with just 62 percent working; of those, half are working part-time jobs.[43] Millennials suffer a real unemployment rate of 16.3 percent[44] and have $1 trillion in student debt.[45] Average incomes for millennials dropped 8 percent[46] since 2007 and their median net worth declined 37 percent between 2005 and 2010.[47] Government economic policy has therefore spectacularly failed the millennial generation.

In July 2014, the Reason Foundation, with support from the Arthur N. Rupe Foundation, conducted a survey and issued its findings in *Millennials: The Politically Unclaimed Generation—The Reason-Rupe Spring 2014 Millennial Survey.*[48] The report is the largest and most comprehensive of its kind, providing fascinating insights into the millennial generation. According to the study, millennials think "government is inefficient, abuses its power, and supports cronyism," with 66 percent of millennials agreeing that government is "inefficient and wasteful," compared with an already skeptical 42 percent in 2009.[49] Since the global financial crisis and the excessive greed and failed policy responses, 63 percent of millennials think government regulations favor special interests, compared with just 18 percent who feel regulators act in the public's interest.[50] Similarly, 58 percent of millennials are convinced government agencies abuse their powers, while only 25 percent trust these same agencies to do the right thing. When the link is made between government, taxation, and value for money, 57 percent of millennials favor "smaller government, providing fewer services, with low taxes."[51] Such distrust of government is understandable considering the economic and political circumstances millennials have lived through.

The Reason-Rupe report also finds that skepticism of government economic intervention has millennials favoring a reduced role for government in their lives. Consistent with these beliefs is the fact that 64 percent of millennials say cutting government spending by 5 percent would help the economy, while 59 percent say cutting taxes would also help the economy.[52] Moreover, 53 percent of millennials believe that reducing the size of government would help the economy and 66 percent believe raising taxes on the wealthy would help the economy.[53] Considering the unintended consequences of government quantitative easing economic policies and the associated rising income inequality in the United States, these results are not the least bit surprising.

According to the Reason-Rupe report, millennials believe that government should help those in need. It is worth noting that millennials' support for all forms of government intervention and redistributive policies vastly decreases as their incomes rise. When millennials start earning between $40,000 and $60,000, they reach a philosophical tipping point at which 40 percent support redistributive policies and only 50 percent support raising taxes.[54] At incomes of greater than $100,000 per year, millennials are far more appalled by the concept of government intervention, with 57 percent opposed to redistributive policies and 53 percent opposed to raising taxes.[55] The data indicates that millennials become far more politically and economically aware as their incomes rise. Their attitudes also demonstrate how ineffective big government has been in their lives. As millennials discover gainful employment, earn greater incomes, and pay higher taxes, their perception toward government shifts dramatically; rather than seeking policies of intervention, they come to believe that government is largely *irrelevant*.

## Not Politics as Usual

As a generation, millennials have been raised in an information-on-demand culture that fosters an expectation of immediate results. Major challenges like dealing with the consequences of the global financial crisis will take years, if not decades, to rectify. Young people were most hopeful of positive change to their financial circumstances when President Barack H. Obama assumed office in 2008. After all, millennial voters accounted for about 3.4 million of the additional 5.4 million national popular voters in 2008, and overwhelmingly voted for Senator Barack H. Obama over Senator John S. McCain by a margin of two to one, or 66 percent to 32 percent, according to the Pew Research Center.[56]

A 2013 Harvard Survey, however, found that 52 percent of younger millennials, those aged eighteen to twenty-four, said they would "recall and replace" President Obama.[57] Evidently, patience is not a virtue of the millennial generation. Politics is about managing expectations, but millennials clearly have a short attention span and expect economic and political results with the same speed and accuracy that they receive Google search results.

Millennials have evolved in a world of almost endless choices, in stark contrast to the less complicated world of fewer choices experienced by their parents. For instance, baby boomers grew up with a choice between Coca-Cola or Pepsi, Republican or Democrat. Whereas millennials go to Starbucks and have more than 87,000 espresso drink combinations alone to choose from![58] Therefore, the notion of adapting to constraints and arbitrary boundaries is anathema to millennials. As a consequence, when faced with a political challenge requiring a unique solution, millennials are more inclined to ask "Why not?" than "Why?" This inherent entrepreneurial spirit, facilitated by a culture of disruptive innovation, has yet to transform a political process characterized by gridlock, inefficiency, and inconsistency, however.

In July 2014, a *New York Post* editorial screamed, "Free the Millennials!," and aptly outlined the looming political battleground of the coming decades.[59] The global financial crisis demonstrated to the millennial generation the enormous economic consequences of big government's excessive market intervention and policy failure. These experiences were formative, formidable, and figurative, and have shaped a generation's philosophical belief system. The ideological challenge for millennials as they emerge as a political force is to embrace the lessons learned from the immense failures of previous political and economic policies.

Millennials tend to articulate a straightforward political philosophy: they want the government out of their bedrooms, bank accounts, and Blackberrys. At the same time, big government policy solutions have made millennials poor, with bleak economic prospects. This generation not only wants the right to determine what occurs in their bedroom, they want the opportunity to *own* their own bedroom and build real wealth during their lifetime. Millennials understand that free markets underwrite the other social freedoms in society, and will therefore seek an alternative political doctrine that facilitates the economic prosperity they lacked while embracing the personal freedoms they cherish. Perhaps that explains the conclusion of the Reason-Rupe report in July 2014 that millennials are "the politically unclaimed generation."[60] Millennials are seeking validation from political leadership that offers positive, uplifting solutions emphasizing upward mobility, inalienable personal liberty, and limitless economic opportunity.

## The American Dream

Millennials have grown up to admire entrepreneurship and self-reliance, and they seek to redefine the concept of prosperity. In the words of *Time* magazine in 2013, "If there's one thing college kids know how to do it's how to bypass conventional institutions and their bureaucracies."[61] As the early adopters of new technology and the trust economy, millennials have embraced a sense of customization in their own lives. This adaptability is important, because in the wake of the global financial crisis the American dream of the baby boomers looked very different, if not unattainable, for millennials.

In fact, in this brave new world of individual economic liberty, the American Dream is now "do-it-yourself," according to the fifth annual MetLife study.[62] According to the study, the new American Dream is "less conventional and more personalized," philosophically driven by individuals who forsake an unrealistic collective vision and prefer instead to build prosperity based on personal values. Interestingly, 59 percent of millennials do not believe home ownership is essential to the American Dream.[63] This shift in perception is important for an economy that has been largely premised on the assumption that wealth is derived primarily from homeownership. This assumption has fuelled the economy over generations, encouraging citizens to invest in real estate and borrow money from banks to realize their ambitions. After the banking failures of 2008, it is understandable that millennials are less convinced of this path to prosperity. The study found that 70 percent of millennials believe being wealthy is also nonessential. In fact, the study found that 53 percent of millennials believe the American Dream is about personal achievement rather than opportunity for all.[64] This indicates a keen sense of economic self-sufficiency whereby millennials value individual rewards based on personal and meritocratic endeavor.

According to a survey by Fidelity Investments conducted in 2013, 17 percent of millennials believe "government failed to do its job" and 24 percent believe that "bankers and lenders were too fixed on making money," and credit these as the causes of the global financial crisis. However, 48 percent of millennials agree that the global financial crisis was due to the fact that "people borrowed more than they could afford."[65] The results are two to one in favor of self-responsibility compared to simply blaming banks for the crisis. In other words, the actions of human beings, including greed and myopic selfishness, were the primary cause of the global financial crisis in the eyes of the millennials surveyed. Considering the economic devastation millennials inherited, it is quite remarkable they are so honest in their appraisal. It would be far easier to apportion blame to the banking sector or government than to accept the critical role citizens played in the crisis.

Furthermore, the disastrous economic conditions faced by millennials could understandably have resulted in more selfishness rather than increased selflessness. This was clearly not the case, as millennials are more willing than any other age group to volunteer their time. Approximately 1.3 million more millennials volunteered their time to nonprofit organizations in 2008 compared with the year before. In fact, the increase of millennials represented the entire gain in volunteerism compared to flat levels of participation for other age groups, according to the Corporation for National and Community Service.[66] By fully embracing the ethical philosophy of enlightened self-interest, millennials are consciously deviating from the myopic selfishness and moral failures of previous generations that caused the economic devastation of the financial crisis.

If the stereotype of millennials holds true, their self-assurance, confidence, and antiestablishment tendencies can be counted as important attributes in a world dominated by economic distress: risk taking and entrepreneurship are vital to sustained economic growth. Millennials, for the most part, possess an indomitable entrepreneurial spirit. After all, they have grown up in a world dominated by constant technological innovation and advancements, and idolizing the likes of college dropouts Steve Jobs and Mark Zuckerberg. In the process of innovating in their fields, figures like Jobs and Zuckerberg have become industry pioneers, inspiring millions of people to embrace change and amassing personal fortunes worth several billion dollars, all without even wearing a suit or tie. This economic antiestablishment mentality, so admired by millennials, has fuelled the evolution of the trust economy and fundamentally reshaped commerce by placing people back at the heart of the economic system.

Millennials will demand economic prosperity as a core component of public policy, reflecting their enlightened self-interest. Millennials overwhelmingly favor a "free market economy" compared to an economy "managed by the government."[67] In fact, the numbers are two to one in favor of free markets. According to the Reason-Rupe report, 64 percent favor economic freedom compared to 32 percent who favor government planning.[68] As time passes and the millennial generation becomes more economically and politically powerful, these values will only grow stronger and more pervasive. This movement may be conscious or it may be unconscious, but it will become an unstoppable economic force once it is fully unleashed.

Freedom of economic opportunity is what millennials desire. By harnessing the power of technology, access to information, and their free market instincts, and drawing on the ethical philosophy of enlightened self-interest, millennials will become the wealthiest, most philanthropic, and most prosperous generation in history. British Prime Minister Benjamin Disraeli once said, "Youth is the trustee of prosperity." Indeed, those words are as true in the twenty-first century as they were in the nineteenth century.

## The Millennial Generation Will Reshape Wall Street

Over the next forty years, the largest intergenerational wealth transfer in history will occur. It is estimated that $41 trillion will transfer from baby boomers to their children and grandchildren.[69] Millennials have grown up amid some of the worst economic circumstances in history, and these events have shaped their philosophical views about the role of business, finance, and investing. The Deloitte *Millennial Survey of 2014* indicated that millennials view the primary role of business as to "improve society," marginally ahead of to "generate profit."[70] It would be naive to assume that millennials will not actively seek to generate market returns with their investments, but the study does indicate that the risk-adjusted returns will be measured against positive social impacts.

By 2020, there will be 103 million millennials in the United States.[71] In five years, they will account for 36 percent of the adult population, 40 percent of eligible voters, and approximately half the workforce. In a decade, millennials will account for 75 percent of the workforce.[72] They are poised to fundamentally re-create corporate America by flexing their economic and political muscle and determining the cultural, philosophical, and financial direction of the country. It is unlikely that millennials will seek economic retribution against the generations before them, but it is highly likely that they will make sure that business, investment, and Wall Street thoroughly understand their role within the economic system and consider their impact on society. This is almost a certainty, because many of these institutions will be managed directly or indirectly by millennials.

Therefore, the entire finance industry is in a state of flux. If Wall Street continues to embrace a culture that fails to recognize its broader impact on society, it is likely millennials will move their money to managers whose values embrace profit with positive social impact. Millennials have a different view about prosperity than their parents do, and they will soon be able to exercise their perspective accordingly. The challenge will be whether Wall Street and the finance industry embrace the changes by actively supporting millennials and their ambitions or continue down the path of the status quo, with scant regard for the business practices or social impacts of their investments and focusing purely on zero-sum profit. Finance is a force for good, and millennials will be the generation that etches the fact into history.

# Chapter 3

# Reimagining Prosperity

It is my belief that all humans share an inherent desire to live a more prosperous life. This phenomenon is articulated by the ethical philosophy of enlightened self-interest, which in economic terms can manifest itself as "doing well by doing good." This concept fundamentally explains why brave entrepreneurs take risks to deliver products and services that society values. Aspen Institute CEO Walter Isaacson said, "Innovation occurs when ripe seeds fall on fertile ground."[1] These bold entrepreneurs include the young women seeking microfinance in Bangladesh. They are the traders in rural China selling whatever they can to survive. They are the kids in Kenya using their mobile phones as a bank. They are the college dropouts in Silicon Valley dreaming of building a better world. They are the real estate moguls in Manhattan wanting to build more housing.

The Internet has democratized the ability to innovate and scale, while free markets have democratized the ability to generate prosperity. Harnessing these two unstoppable forces in the service of good represents a truly remarkable antidote to forces of evil and oppression. Success is measured by the ability of these entrepreneurial concepts to satisfy the needs of others in society. Wealth and prosperity flow to buyer and seller in the marketplace, enriching the entire community. Tyranny is evil, and so is poverty. The global financial crisis is a real-time case study in ethical, moral, and government policy failure. The economic collapse of numerous welfare states across Europe merely reinforces that government does a manifestly inadequate job of private wealth creation. Therefore, it is the private sector, empowered by free markets and embracing enlightened self-interest, that shares the responsibility to repair the broken world by reimagining prosperity and creating opportunities for all people who dream of a better world. Finance has the power to make these dreams become reality.

## Importance of Economic Growth

The Golden Rule—do unto others as you would have others do unto you—describes a relationship between one's self and others that involves both sides equally. It is an age-old ethical concept of reciprocity that has application in a variety of cultures, and enlightened self-interest vis-à-vis capitalism can be interpreted as the economic application of the Golden Rule. The ethical philosophy of enlightened self-interest structurally underpins the basis for capitalism, and explains why economic freedom results in greater economic development for all. Freedom enables people to specialize in the things they are good at and allows countries to trade. Free trade lets nations sell resources they have a comparative advantage in producing and buy resources from other nations that have superior alternatives. As trade grows, national wealth increases, and employment and self-reliance increase as well. Living standards rise and prosperity flows. Free markets have lifted more people out of poverty than anything else, ever. In fact, there has been no greater force for good in the history of humankind.

Economic growth is by far the best way to fight poverty. The World Bank estimates that 80 percent of poverty reduction is due to economic growth,[2] and strong growth during the quarter century between 1981 and 2005 lifted a billion people out of extreme poverty. The World Bank estimated that extreme poverty halved, dropping from 42 percent to 21 percent during that twenty-five-year time period, and predicts that extreme poverty will continue to fall to 11 percent in 2020.[3] The World Bank defines extreme poverty as incomes in the developing world of $1.25 a day or less.[4]

At the Georgetown Global Social Enterprise Initiative in 2012, U2 lead singer and antipoverty activist Bono said, "Entrepreneurial capitalism takes more people out of poverty than aid."[5] That was a ringing endorsement from a man who has spent decades appealing for greater government foreign aid and is better known for singing greatest hits than singing the praises of capitalism. Free markets not only deliver reductions in poverty but also higher incomes. Unsurprisingly, countries with the highest economic growth are also countries with the fastest income growth among the poor. This enables people at the bottom of the economic pyramid to purchase an increased quality and quantity of food. According to the United Nations, people now consume significantly more fruit, vegetables, and protein, reducing undernourishment rates among children in developing countries from 31 percent in 1990 to 26 percent in 2008.[6] The World Bank estimates daily calorie intake rose from 2,200 per person in 1960 to 2,800 in 2007.[7] Many of the world's poorest people are agricultural farmers, so increased food consumption and free trade have had a positive impact on their living standards.

Rising living standards have had widespread political ramifications as well. Free markets are the natural precursor to a whole range of other personal freedoms, because capitalism is the economic equivalent of free speech. Dictatorships are more likely to democratize as they become richer, and democracies are less likely to collapse the richer they grow. There is an exception to this rule, however, specifically in countries that are endowed with oil resources, where there is a tendency toward ruthless dictatorship and hereditary monarchical concentration of power. According to the International Monetary Fund, forty-five of the fifty-six countries with gross domestic product per capita exceeding $15,000 are democracies. Therefore, rich countries more often than not also tend to be robustly free societies.[8]

Perhaps even more telling is the data from the Cato Institute's Annual Economic Freedom of the World Index.[9] In 2011, countries that fall into the top quartile of the measurement for economic freedom had an average per capita income of $36,446, compared with $4,382 for countries in the bottom quartile. Interestingly, the average income of the poorest 10 percent of the top quartile was $10,556, more than double the overall average income of the bottom quartile.[10] In other words, the freer a nation is, the richer it becomes. Political and civil liberties are considerably higher in economically free nations than in politically repressive and tyrannical nations. As a result, life expectancy is 79.2 years in countries in the top quartile of economic freedom compared to 60.2 years in the bottom quartile.[11] Nobel Laureate Milton Friedman once made the point that, "the only cases in which the masses have escaped from grinding poverty in recorded history, are where they have had capitalism and largely free trade. If you want to know where the masses are worst off, it's exactly in the kind of societies that depart from that."[12]

## Role of Government

The Gettysburg Address, delivered by President Abraham Lincoln on the afternoon of Thursday, November 19, 1863,[13] came to be regarded as one of the greatest speeches in American history. In it, he reiterated the principles of human equality enshrined in the Declaration of Independence and he proclaimed the Civil War a struggle for the preservation of the Union.[14] He also advocated for the principle of human equality with "a new birth of freedom"[15] that would bring true equality to all of the country's citizens.[16] Lincoln also reminded his audience that the United States was founded on the premise of government "of the people, by the people, and for the people."

The founding fathers of the United States were political leaders and statesmen who helped birth a new nation by signing the Declaration of Independence, serving in the Revolutionary War, and establishing the United States Constitution. The Declaration of Independence famously gives three examples of "unalienable Rights" that were "endowed by their Creator" and include, "Life, Liberty and the pursuit of Happiness."[17] Free markets based on the ethical philosophy of enlightened self-interest are the economic expression of that liberty. The United States' economy is therefore based on the capitalist system empowering individual economic and political freedom of choice. America was established to fundamentally foster the very best of human achievement.

Therefore, the founding fathers held a view, enshrined in the principles outlined in the Declaration of Independence and the United States Constitution, that the role of government should be limited, in the sense that the system ought to be constructed with a set of checks and balances. Moreover, government would not be run like a business to generate profit, but the government role should be proportionately sized relative to its share of economic activity so as not to stifle private-sector creativity. As with the running of any organization, it becomes necessary to collect money from the people in the form of taxation to fund government programs. As the size and scope of government increases, it becomes necessary to raise taxes to collect more revenue. As government grows, it becomes necessary to collect a much greater share of wealth from the middle class, the socioeconomic term for the broad group of people in contemporary society who fall between the working class and the wealthy. As the size of government grows, the middle class naturally becomes the obvious target, as the poor tend not to pay any federal income tax.

Since the global financial crisis, the private sector in the United States has been crowded out by the massive expansion of government. According to the Congressional Budget Office, in 2008 the size of the United States Federal Budget was $2.98 trillion, and had grown over 25 percent, to $3.72 trillion, in 2013.[18] In 2008, federal spending was 20.8 percent of gross domestic product and grew to 23.3 percent by 2013. During this period, the compound annual growth rate for federal spending was 5.2 percent, nearly three times the rate of inflation. In addition, federal debt held by the public increased to $13.3 trillion, equivalent to 80.4 percent of gross domestic product.[19]

As the size of government grows unchecked, it creates the "crowding out effect,"[20] where increased government spending replaces, or drives down, private-sector investment. Government is not a wealth-creating vehicle, nor has it ever been successful when it has tried to be. The private sector is able to do things government simply cannot, because it is unconstrained by the bureaucratic inefficiency of collectivism, short-term electoral cycles, and a limited pool of human capital. In a free market economy, the private sector is where individuals and corporations provide the goods and services that generate employment, economic growth, and prosperity.

In February 2013, *Crunch Time: Fiscal Crises and the Role of Monetary Policy* was published for the U.S. Monetary Policy Forum in New York City. The paper stated that, "Countries with debt above 80 per cent of G.D.P. and persistent current-account deficits are vulnerable to a rapid fiscal deterioration as a result of these tipping-point dynamics."[21] *New York Times* reporter Binyamin Appelbaum published an article in response to the paper's conclusion, titled "Predicting a Crisis, Repeatedly."[22] The article explained that, "This [analysis] is bad news for the United States because, as it happens, the national debt is 80 percent of annual economic output, the nation has a persistent current-account deficit, and it is planning to significantly increase the scale of borrowing, relative to output, in coming decades."[23] The article went on to say, "the bottom line is always the same: the federal debt cannot continue to grow relative to the size of the economy, or else investors will start demanding much higher interest rates and the United States will fall into crisis."[24]

Based on findings of the report presented to the U.S. Monetary Policy Forum, a one percentage point increase in debt as a share of gross domestic product increases ten-year borrowing costs by 4.5 basis points. This equates to an additional $450,000 in annual interest payments for every $1 billion in extra debt.[25] Furthermore, a one percentage point increase in the current account deficit raises borrowing costs by 18 basis points or the equivalent of $1.8 million in interest for every $1 billion in debt.[26] So, debt levels that cross thresholds estimated to be 80 percent debt to gross domestic product can result in investors demanding significantly higher interest rates.

It is immaterial whether the tipping point for the United States is 80 percent debt to GDP or any other higher number. Countries with more debt run a greater risk of losing investor confidence, reducing their credit rating, and crushing the confidence of the job-creating private sector. The U.S. debt predicament also limits its flexibility to deal effectively with new or unforeseen economic problems. According to Jerome H. Powell, a Federal Reserve governor quoted in the *New York Times* piece, "We don't know where the tipping point is." But, he continued, "Wherever it is, we're getting closer to it."[27] The global economy, with record-low interest rates, remains weak in the wake of the global financial crisis. It is difficult to see how robust growth can occur if that kind of debt cycle begins because it can be very hard to escape.

In general terms, higher government debts mean higher taxes to service the interest payments. Higher taxes have a depressing effect on the economy. This subsequent government expansion is an impediment to economic growth and acts as a headwind for continued human economic prosperity. If the United States reaches a tipping point, whereby more people require assistance from government than are financially contributing toward it, the country will gradually descend into an abysmal cycle of poverty. This may take several years or even decades to transpire, but unless the balance is renegotiated toward an economy that is self-sufficient, the trend will be terminal. Therefore, the private sector needs to step up to the plate and reestablish itself as the engine of the economy and prosperity.

## To Get Rich Is Glorious

Capitalism creates preconditions for earned success to flourish in the economic sphere. Empowered by the philosophy of enlightened self-interest, entrepreneurs take risks and create businesses small or large, essentially making something out of nothing. This act hopefully generates employment for others, as well as a sense of dignity, self-worth, and increased marginal utility. If the business is successful it generates profits in addition to the satisfaction of achievement. The role of government is not to restrict this process, but rather to establish a setting in which this ecosystem can thrive. Where government intervenes unnecessarily, it only erects barriers to entry, which enables existing participants in the marketplace to restrict competition and encourages inefficient business practices. This, in turn, stifles entrepreneurship, employment, human development, and economic growth. Only private-sector entrepreneurs harnessing the immense power of free markets can generate sustainable economic growth and deliver prosperity.

The United States and many other countries are saddled with record government debt, enormous unfunded liabilities, and massive underemployment. The only way out of this malaise is to grow out of it. Sustainable economic growth is the only solution to the enormous economic and social challenges the world faces in the dark shadow of the global financial crisis. In simple terms, the economy needs to get bigger, *much bigger*. Economic growth since the economic crisis that began in 2008 has been restricted by the false perception that free markets have failed, and thus global growth has declined despite the vast increases in government spending in developed economies. The irony is that businesses in free markets must, by definition, be allowed to fail. In a free market, economic benefits flow efficiently to where demand and supply intersect. If there is a disconnection between the two curves, there is no equilibrium point. Therefore, where there is no market, inefficient or unprofitable businesses fail. Creative destruction and competition are vitally important for the continued survival of the human race. In 2008, capitalism did not fail. Rather, human beings failed by deviating from the path of enlightened self-interest toward near-terminal myopic selfishness.

The spread of the best of capitalism throughout the world has, however, had a profoundly greater global impact than the perils of the global financial crisis had. Over the last century, prosperity underpinned by free markets and capitalism has been warmly embraced in the Western world. Over just the last quarter century, capitalism has also helped to raise more than a billion people out of poverty. In China alone, more than 680 million people have been rescued from poverty, and the extreme poverty rate has gone from 84 percent in 1980 to less than 10 percent today.[28] While China remains a totalitarian state, a great number of citizens have benefited tremendously in economic and social terms with the introduction of selected free market economic opportunities that allow them to pursue private enterprise and create wealth.

Deng Xiaoping, revolutionary statesman and political leader, has been referred to as the "paramount leader" of the People's Republic of China and "the chief architect of China's economic reforms and China's socialist modernization."[29] In the spring of 1992, Deng made his famous tour of southern China, delivering speeches that generated large local support for his reformist platform. Deng stressed the importance of economic reforms in China and uttered the famous catchphrase, "To get rich is glorious," unleashing a wave of personal entrepreneurship that continues to drive China's economy today.[30] People in the West have mistakenly interpreted Deng's statement as solely in reference to wealth creation, however it is a much broader reference to the importance of happiness, consistent with the teachings of Chinese philosopher Confucius.[31] In fact, *new Confucianism* is a distinct product of China's economic reforms, particularly the capitalist triumphalism of the Deng Xiaoping era.[32] This is akin to the doctrine of the "pursuit of happiness" espoused in the U.S. Declaration of Independence.[33]

Even the Chinese Communist Party, the ruling political party of the People's Republic of China, has recognized that private enterprise can achieve things government cannot. Human development and wealth creation are inextricably linked because abundant prosperity benefits the entire society. According to the Pew Research Center, 76 percent of Chinese agree that most people are better off in a free market economy.[34] By way of comparison, the same study showed that only 70 percent of Americans agreed.[35] In 2014, there are more than one billion capitalists in China, more than in any other nation on earth. This data indicates that China has learned economic lessons from the United States, and has so far avoided some of the pitfalls that have been associated with economic growth, such as excessive greed and myopic selfishness. The ethical philosophy of enlightened self-interest has delivered so much prosperity and opportunity to the developing world that it is remarkable so many people in the developed world deny the success of the capitalist system.

The global financial crisis has indeed brought about a profound economic helplessness for millions of people in developed economies, and may well bequeath to the next generation a life of poverty and chronic unemployment. In July 2012, the *Wall Street Journal* published an article by Charles Murray titled, "Why Capitalism Has an Image Problem."[36] According to the article, being a capitalist has "become an accusation." Moreover, "The creative destruction that is at the heart of a growing economy is now seen as evil. Americans increasingly appear to accept the mind-set that kept the world in poverty for millennia: If you've gotten rich, it is because you made someone else poorer."[37] This anti-freedom mentality is destroying the notion of enlightened self-interest as the core moral philosophy in markets. In so doing, it stifles entrepreneurship among the very people who have the most to gain from increasing economic development and wealth creation. Millennials have been bequeathed a terrible set of economic circumstances and are core constituents in the quest to reimagine prosperity.

The trust economy has played an important role at the grassroots level by dispelling some of the unfavorable myths about free markets. It will take time for the understanding to filter through that technological advancements can only occur in a free market. In many respects, entrepreneurs empowered by the trust economy represent the best of free market capitalism because they place individuals at the core of the system. According to Brian Chesky, CEO of Airbnb, "This is a new economy, the sharing economy," making reference to the revolutionary changes taking place in commerce because of disruptive innovation businesses.[38] At a press conference in San Francisco in November 2013, Chesky went further by saying, "There are laws for people and laws for business, but you are a new category—people as businesses."[39] It is worth noting that Brian Chesky is officially part of the millennial generation.[40] His enthusiasm for a more prosperous world concluded with, "It's actually starting to feel like a revolution."[41] The United States has always been a nation that idolizes entrepreneurs who embody the essence of risk taking, like Thomas Edison, Henry Ford, and Bill Gates. Businesses and entrepreneurs in the trust economy represent a new paradigm for capitalism in the U.S., a paradigm in which trade and commerce benefit individuals directly rather than large multinational corporations. Entrepreneurs acting within the ethical bounds of enlightened self-interest have enabled people everywhere to become richer, freer, and happier by providing a platform for more efficient consumption.

As capitalism has been exported, the living standards for billions of people across the world have irretrievably risen. Capitalism enabled the world economy to experience exponential growth, with private-sector entrepreneurs generating goods and services that consumers need and receiving economic benefits that appropriately compensate them for the financial risks they took to establish those businesses. This allows more brave entrepreneurs to invest in new ideas, create additional employment, promote research and development, and encourage innovation. This, in turn, fosters a competitive environment in which others seek to create new and better products, opening up new markets and achieving greater success. Incentives in a free market provide the opportunity for people to achieve their boundless potential and make the world a more enjoyable place to live. Free markets have created hope and opportunity by promoting the fundamental human desire to live a more prosperous life. In this endeavor, reimagining prosperity means applauding success and abundance by embracing enlightened self-interest and channeling the words of Deng Xiaoping.

## The Private Sector and Public Policy

According to the Organisation for Economic Co-operation and Development, of the one hundred largest global economies as measured by GDP in 2000, fifty-one were corporations and forty-nine were nation states.[42] In addition, revenues of the one hundred largest corporations equalled roughly 20 percent of world's gross domestic product. [43] In the post-crisis world, there are corporations that have measurably stronger balance sheets than many Western governments. For example, Apple Corporation had a market capitalization of over $450 billion, with more than $160 billion cash on its balance sheet in April 2014.[44] At the same time, Microsoft Corporation had a market capitalization of over $330 billion, with more than $85 billion cash on its balance sheet.[45] Based on figures compiled by Bank of America and US Trust, the *Telegraph* in London published an article in April 2014 titled, "Apple and Microsoft Have Bigger Cash Holdings Than UK."[46] Apple had three times as much cash on hand as the United States Treasury at the time, which had only $49 billion on hand to keep the government working, according to *Forbes*.[47] The figures were calculated by analyzing company filings, financial metrics from Moody's Corporation, and data from the International Monetary Fund. Other companies with large amounts of cash on hand included Google, with $58 billion, Verizon Communications, with $53 billion, and Cisco Systems, with $46 billion. The combined cash reserves of Apple, Microsoft, Google, Verizon, and Pfizer stood at $400 billion by the end of 2013.[48]

These private-sector corporations are unrestricted by sovereign boundaries or political mandate, as governments must be. Furthermore, some of these corporations have global operations spanning multiple jurisdictions, which gives them the capacity to allocate resources expeditiously and scale programs across their internal human capital networks. Therefore, these private-sector corporations have the capacity to implement strategies, including enlightened public policy, without the need for government decree. In fact, private corporations can be more effective at implementing public policy than government.

Health care has been a divisive public policy issue in the United States for many decades. Following years of well-intentioned debate about the problems and alternative solutions, the health-care sector in the U.S. had grown to over $2.8 trillion in 2012. In fact, costs had risen exponentially without commensurate medical benefits or increases in life expectancy.[49] At the same time, the major public-policy debate was heavily focused on health-care reform. In 2010, President Obama signed into law the Affordable Care Act, a federal overhaul of regulations that sought to provide Americans with access to health insurance, aiming especially to cover the poor and difficult-to-insure segment of the population. The goal of the plan was to expand the affordability, availability, and quality of private and public health insurance through a combination of consumer protections, subsidies, and insurance exchanges.

At the same time, in 2012, Walmart employed 2.1 million people around the world and was the largest private-sector employer in the United States.[50] Walmart operates more than 4,800 stores across the U.S. and Puerto Rico, receiving 150 million customer visits per week.[51] Putting the Walmart behemoth in perspective, there are 130 million visits to American hospital departments every year.[52] Recognizing that each employee and customer requires health care in some form, Walmart set an ambitious goal of becoming the leading health-insurance provider in the retail industry.[53]

According to a study by the *Washington Examiner*, Walmart is able to offer its full-time employees a more affordable health-care plan with greater coverage than they could find on the insurance exchanges set up under the Affordable Care Act.[54] The study indicated that a hypothetical thirty-year-old smoker earning $30,000 per year would pay a $70 monthly health-care premium under the Walmart plan. This compared favorably to a $352 monthly premium, with subsidies, under an estimate for the nationwide average silver plan available under the Affordable Care Act.[55] Despite the best intention of government, this is an example of the private sector providing a more affordable, efficient, and preferable outcome than the government alternative. It demonstrates a model for other major corporations to follow that reduces pressure on scarce public resources, and shows that solutions driven by the private sector can be immensely successful in meeting a whole host of public policy challenges, including the important issue of employee health care. In 1992, the United Nations Conference on Environment and Development was held in Rio de Janeiro, Brazil. Also known as the Earth Summit, the conference included 172 participating governments, of which 116 sent their head of state.[56] At the summit there were many ambitious multilateral environmental initiatives discussed relating to international environmental outcomes. Some twenty years later, in 2012, the United Nations again held a conference in Rio de Janeiro, Brazil, called RIO+20, denoting the two decades since the original summit. Unfortunately for the environment, it was a wasted twenty years marked by inertia as well as a lack of accountability and environmental arbitrage among nation-states. Throughout this prolonged period of missed opportunity, corporations have been far more effective than governments in implementing meaningful environmental public policy solutions.

Water is a major input cost in the coffee supply chain and a vital global resource that is being depleted quickly. Starbucks Corporation, a $16 billion-a-year business in 2014, has approximately twenty thousand stores operating in more than sixty countries.[57] Starbucks directly and indirectly consumes hundreds of millions of gallons of water each year, a greater water usage than some small countries. Recognizing a financial incentive to reduce input costs, in 2008 Starbucks voluntarily decided to reduce water consumption by 25 percent in company-owned stores by 2015. In addition to the financial benefits of the company realized by reducing water consumption, there were also measurable environmental benefits for society. Starbucks' model corporate behavior has had a positive impact on the environment, as it has utilized its scale and been willing to collaborate and innovate with other stakeholders to reduce water consumption and improve the environment. This has led other companies to promote similar environmental sustainability initiatives that are measurable, meaningful, and enforceable, a far more effective means of implementing enlightened environmental public policy outcomes than the impotent global government efforts.

Multilateral government environmental policy has largely been a failure due to the symbolic, rather than practical, application of various environmental strategies outlined in frameworks like the

Kyoto Protocol. Specifically, the academic-led policy response has largely focused on redistributive tax policies rather than real environmental solutions. Nobel Laureate Milton Friedman once said, "The repeated failure of well-intentioned programs is not an accident. The failure is deeply rooted in the use of bad means to achieve good objectives."[58] Corporations would achieve far more environmentally advantageous outcomes if they explicitly disclosed energy costs, for example, in their annual reports. As a result, corporations would be held financially accountable for another expense line item on the balance sheet, and market pressures would force leadership to seek to reduce costs, as with any other expense item. Therefore, corporations would lower energy costs, which would most certainly correlate with more energy-efficient consumption strategies like using less energy or cheaper energy. Moreover, lower energy use means lower carbon emissions, and the United Nations claims emissions are harming the environment. This single market-led outcome would have more positive environmental impact than any government-imposed regulation would.

Private-sector corporations have the power to positively improve the state of the world when their leadership pursues the corporate ethical equivalent of enlightened self-interest. Good corporate citizenship also demonstrates the superior ability of private-sector entities to implement real public-policy outcomes in a far more effective way than the inefficient public sector. It is important to quantify these activities in a measurable and accountable fashion, providing the financial justification for the provision of services beyond pure profit-generating activities. Corporate social responsibility has therefore become an important function of large private-sector corporations, to systematically aggregate and effectively communicate the positive social benefits of their business activities. The private sector is demonstrably better equipped to deliver public-policy outcomes than government, and the private sector creates the conditions that lead to a fundamentally preferable vision for a more prosperous world. In order for the private sector to thrive, there needs to be access to robust and affordable financial capital to make the investments necessary for entrepreneurs and small businesses to grow in the marketplace. This underscores the vital importance of the banking and finance industry in facilitating the growth of the private sector.

## Doing Well by Doing Good

The global financial crisis provided a platform that allowed the enemies of free markets to have their day in the sun attacking wealth creation, banking, and capitalism. These people are no different from those who exercised egregious moral and ethical failure in the lead-up to 2008. In fact, the same critics have forgotten the essence of enlightened self-interest as the core basis for human interaction, placing people at the heart of the capitalist system as the philosophical foundation for free markets. Critics of free markets argue that the financial system is too large and overly complex, requiring government intervention to reduce its size and scope. This is an overly simplistic and juvenile debate to have about an economy the size of the United States', which comprises one-fifth of the world economy. Furthermore, the banking sector plays an important role by facilitating the provision of private credit within the economy, thus enabling businesses to invest, innovate, employ, and generate economic growth. This drives increased living standards and greater prosperity for all citizens.

The question ought to be asked, why do some people hate free markets? The moral compass has swung too far if those who are driven to provide the capital to fund innovative ideas are demonized. The role of the banking and financial sector is perhaps the most important in the entire economy. Finance is about matching ideas with capital and matching capital with great ideas. It is fundamentally about progress, not regress. Free markets are philosophically about making the hopes and dreams of risk-taking entrepreneurs become reality. This is a moral issue, where the role of the private sector is to promote human development and prosperity. Free markets empowered by people pursuing the ethical philosophy of enlightened self-interest are, by and large, the primary solution to the troubling economic circumstances in the world rather than the cause.

In 2009, Goldman Sachs chief executive Lloyd C. Blankfein was quoted in the *Times* of London as saying, "We help companies to grow by helping them to raise capital. Companies that grow create wealth. This, in turn, allows people to have jobs that create more growth and more wealth. It's a virtuous cycle."[59] Blankfein is absolutely correct when he asserts, "We should educate the public more about how business and its core activities have lifted people out of poverty."[60] Furthermore, the only way for the economy to rebuild after the devastation of the global financial crisis is for the private sector to facilitate the further provision of financial capital, enabling businesses to grow and generate employment, raise living standards, and restore hope for billions of people. Indeed, what could be a more noble profession than providing the vital financial capital that enables entrepreneurs to turn their innovations into thriving small businesses?

Banking is the unique purveyor of this gift to society, and banking as a career path ought to be an aspiration for the most talented graduates. It is an immense privilege to work in an industry in which a decision made can be the difference between retirement with financial independence and the need to continue working. Such decisions can mean that the excess profits of a successful enterprise or wealthy industrialist fund philanthropic endowment. When humans are at the center of the economic system and have the freedom to choose, there is no greater moral or ethical guarantor of prosperity than capitalism. At this point in history, the 7.15 billion people living on the planet are deeply interconnected, and people are reimagining prosperity based on ethical principles premised on shared values and mutual success.

# Chapter 4

# Investing with Impact

Making money *and* doing good for society are efforts that are completely intertwined. In fact, the relationship between the two is inherently symbiotic because it is not possible to successfully achieve one without achieving the other. Matching great ideas with the financial resources to make them reality is paramount in the continued circular flow of human development. There is no greater dividend of human achievement than living in abundant prosperity. Of course, prosperity means so much more than dollars and cents. It means a successful, flourishing, and thriving condition, the full force of which manifests itself in abundance. Ultimately, financial investments have an enormous impact on society at large. In a financial sense, successful investments can result in subsequent prosperity and abundance, however, the full impact of investment is often felt far beyond mere financial returns printed on an investment portfolio statement. What lies behind the numbers are people. Investments have the power to positively or negatively impact the human condition. Therefore, creating wealth that benefits society as a whole is the ultimate *noble cause*. In fact, human prosperity depends on it.

Unfortunately, malinvestments[1] and misallocation of resources have distorted this fundamental premise, resulting in adverse consequences and distrust of the entire financial system. The global financial crisis demonstrated that human beings acting with myopic selfishness and excessive greed, and who have vast access to financial resources, can have tremendous negative impact. Furthermore, the assumption that somehow the entire banking and finance industry is broken is unfair and incorrect. After all, the industry is incentivized to deliver positive financial returns to shareholders. The philosophy of enlightened self-interest and the capitalist system place people at the core of the system, which means that financial returns are positively correlated to the satisfaction, or utility, of human beings. Investing with impact means positively influencing the allocation of capital with the intention of achieving measurable outcomes that benefit society. Therefore, the misconception that achieving profits and positive social impact are in some way mutually exclusive must be debunked for the good of humanity.

Philanthropy refers, literally, to the love of humanity, but its financial reach is limited due to the basic constraints of charitable giving and depletion of finite economic resources. Investment, on the other hand, if successful, generates more financial resources, which amplify impact and grow the pie. Ultimately, the profits generated in one part of society underwrite nonprofit activities in other parts. Therefore, more profits can also mean more philanthropic giving opportunities. Finance is fundamentally a force for good in the world because it provides the resources to empower hopes and realize dreams, by delivering abundance and ensuring continued human prosperity.

## Impact Investing

Impact investing is the investment approach that intentionally seeks to achieve positive financial return and generate measurable social impact. The term "impact investing" was first conceived at a meeting of investors at the Rockefeller Bellagio Conference Center in 2007.[2] According to Antony Bugg-Levine, coauthor of *Impact Investing: Transforming How We Make Money While Making a Difference,* the term's dual meaning sought to capture the distinct views among meeting participants.[3] Specifically, there were those who believed that capitalism and the financial system were effective enough to unlock capital for social impact, while others believed that capitalism and the financial system were unsustainable and required radical reform. The language of impact investing deliberately embraces a wide range of perspectives, capturing incrementalists and radicals alike and ensuring that a diversity of opinion shapes the sector.

Impact investing is a term disliked by many, including this author, because it implies that only a subgroup of the investment community is having positive social impact. Simply put, the fact that *every* investment has impact means that we ought to be thinking about all investments through the lens of achieving positive social impact alongside financial performance, rather than expecting that outcome from only a small subsection of the investment landscape. By implication, the traditional or mainstream investment community has neutral, negligible, or negative social impact. This idea is self-fulfilling, and only galvanized the status quo belief among many in the finance community that the investment industry should focus on delivering positive financial returns and nothing else. The inference is that the traditional finance industry has lost its ability to robustly articulate the virtues of profit-based endeavors and almost quarantines mainstream investments from the responsibility of achieving any form of positive social impact. My argument is that investing with a mind-set of achieving impact simultaneously with profit should be the rule, not the exception.

Indeed, if mainstream investors were more cognizant of the social impact of their investments, be it positive or negative, then it's fair to wonder whether the impact investment industry would exist. In other words, if investors thought deeply about the full social impact of investment in companies like Coca-Cola, Starbucks, or Bank of America in the same way they look at a social impact bond or investment in a water project in Africa, then capital would be allocated significantly differently. In other words, company boards and chief executives would be inclined to fully consider the social impact of business decisions because of pressure from investors. Furthermore, it is obvious that free market capitalism is the ultimate impact investment approach because it has delivered an immeasurable positive social impact, offered significant financial returns, and lifted more than a billion people out of extreme poverty.

The finance industry as a whole must start remembering these facts and realigning its belief system accordingly, because myopic selfishness has become too deeply ingrained at the expense of enlightened self-interest, which is best articulated by the impact investing philosophy. Impact investing is about positively influencing the allocation of financial capital and recognizing the forest from the trees, in the sense that an investor can consciously deliver profit and positive social impact.

## Limitations

The definition of impact investing is limited because it means different things to different people. In its broadest sense, impact investing is a wide-ranging investment approach rather than a specific asset class. This has effectively restricted the growth of the industry, constraining its capacity to deliver on said objectives of delivering positive social impact and financial returns. Status quo thinking implies that the investment industry has as its sole responsibility delivering profit and positive financial returns. Clarifying the relationship between profit and positive social impact—in fact articulating that profit and positive social impact are intertwined—has the effect of creating a far more widespread adoption of positive investment practices than the current impact investment mode delivers. Chilean filmmaker, playwright, and author Alejandro Jodorowsky once said, "Birds born in a cage think flying is an illness."[4] Removing the delineation between investing for profit and investing for social good enables vast sources of global financial capital to flow to impact investing. Therefore, measurable outcomes that have a positive social impact can extend across an entire investment portfolio without financial returns being sacrificed.

If impact investing is too narrowly focused on delivering social impact and fails to articulate a coherent investment case, it will fail to attract investment capital. Therein lies the core challenge, because those in the impact investment industry will become just as morally deficient as those who focus exclusively on profit at all costs; the investment thesis needs to be robust, or capital will flow elsewhere. Balancing these two values is about finding the sensible center. In order to create a world in which impact investing has the same mainstream appeal that traditional value investing has, there needs to be a tectonic shift in the mind-set of investors across the spectrum. In this world, there would be fewer people imprisoned, healthier children, a cleaner environment, improved infrastructure, and more efficient governments. In this world, investors would also be earning above-market returns, allowing them to sleep more peacefully at night. The argument that this type of outcome is unachievable is false. Impact investments have already delivered positive social impact in these areas without jeopardizing financial returns—there are examples across the spectrum, including the growth of investors financing green bonds to fund environmental projects.

Value investing is the term applied to the investment approach in which investors seek profit by buying securities at a price that does not reflect the intrinsic value of the underlying investment. This investment approach was originally devised by Benjamin Graham and later popularized by Berkshire Hathaway chairman

Warren Buffett.[5] Impact investing, in contrast, is an investment approach that seeks to achieve measurable results beyond purely financial returns. In other words, the value of an investment may include nonfinancial metrics. By exploring this relationship in more depth, we can see that value investing creates impact and impact investing creates value. However different these two investment approaches may initially appear, value investing and impact investing have a great deal in common.

According to a report released by the World Economic Forum in 2013, the impact investment market is currently estimated to be between $25 and $40 billion.[6] This is a miniscule figure in comparison to the much broader multitrillion-dollar mainstream investment market. In fact, the S&P 500 Index had 187 companies with a total market capitalization greater than or equal to $25 billion in October 2014.[7] At the Berkshire Hathaway Annual Meeting in 2014, chairman Warren Buffett, often described as the "Oracle of Omaha," said, "If we see a really good $50 billion deal, we'll figure out a way to do it."[8] This statement demonstrates the relative scale of traditional investment when compared with the burgeoning impact investment industry; it also demonstrates the importance that traditional and mainstream investors place on generating profit, as Berkshire Hathaway has consistently delivered to its investors. This is the challenge for impact investing: to build a robust investment track record over time that can attract mainstream investment capital while at the same time achieving measurable positive social impact. In fact, it will be a monumental day when the total impact investment capital pool is greater than the bite-size of the next Berkshire Hathaway acquisition.

According to *Forbes*, in 2014 Warren Buffett was fourth on the list of the world's billionaires, with an estimated net worth of $58.2 billion.[9] At the time, much publicity surrounded the announcement, by a company backed by Buffett, to offer a $1 billion reward to the individual who correctly predicted the full suite of college basketball results. Officially known as the "Quicken Loans Billion Dollar Bracket," the competition would award a billion-dollar bounty to any person who could pick the winners of all sixty-three games in the NCAA men's college basketball tournament. The statistical probability of winning this unique challenge was estimated at one in 9,223,372,036,854,775,808, or one in 9.2 quintillion, according to DePaul University math professor Jeff Bergen.[10] Unsurprisingly, nobody won the challenge.[11] But imagine if Warren Buffett, the man regarded by some as the world's greatest investor,[12] had used that same billion dollars to challenge the government of his home state of Nebraska. The money could have been used to structure a social impact bond designed to raise the education standards of minority elementary school students struggling with math, reading, and science.

Also known as a "pay-for-success bond," a social impact bond is defined by Social Finance, Ltd, in the United Kingdom as "based on a commitment from government to use a proportion of the savings that result from improved social outcomes to reward non-government investors that fund the early intervention activities."[13] In 2014, Nebraska's Department of Education reported that only 54 percent of black students demonstrated proficiency in reading, compared to the average of 77 percent for all students. Forty-seven percent of Hispanic students were proficient in science, compared to the average of 70 percent for all students.[14] Closing this gap is a win-win because research suggests that increasing education standards benefits society as a whole. In this example, the private sector would provide initial financial capital for programs aimed specifically at improving the proficiency of minority children in reading and science. The money could be used to fund extra classes, extra teachers, or smaller class sizes, and the metrics for improved proficiency rates based on standardized testing results would be agreed upon in advance. If the standards are not achieved, the private-sector capital is at risk. However, if the standards are achieved, private investors receive an agreed interest rate, or coupon, for the capital invested in the social impact bond.

The savings accrued to Nebraska taxpayers would effectively be redistributed to private investors in the form of their investment return. In contrast to traditional investments that focus exclusively on financial returns, social impact bonds generate substantial and measurable positive social impact. Importantly, these positive social outcomes are complementary to the positive financial returns generated by social impact bonds. For our hypothetical social impact bond, the theory is this: smarter children earn higher incomes later in life, leading to increasing entrepreneurship and risk taking to build small businesses. This subsequently generates profits, leading to greater employment opportunities and more people in the workforce, which delivers greater tax revenues to society as a whole. Raising education standards saves the state vital resources on remedial education costs, reduces poverty, saves on welfare costs, and hopefully decreases crime and, therefore, prison costs. Children win, Nebraska wins, and private investors win. Such an investment is intended to unlock deep intrinsic value, demonstrating that impact investing could really be the new value investing. This is an example of how the mainstream investment community can use finance to fulfill its potential as a great force for good.

## Trillion-Dollar Market Opportunity

Impact investing is a trillion-dollar frontier market ripe for exploitation by astute asset managers who are able to recognize the sheer scale of the opportunity. In fact, the impact investing landscape is perhaps the only scalable part of the investment universe that has yet to be conquered. Morgan Stanley estimates that more than $3.07 trillion, or $1 in $8, of assets under management in the United States follow strategies that "consider corporate responsibility and societal concerns."[15] Therefore, using baseline data from the World Economic Forum of an impact investing market of between $25 billion and $40 billion, there is potential for astonishing growth in the marketplace.[16] Rational observation of the two data points indicate that the delta, or the difference between the two numbers, is a 75 to 125 times growth multiple in the total size of the impact investment market. Furthermore, this market is global in nature, unregulated, opaque, and primed to explode. There remains a staggering opportunity to make the market in this area by building investment products that can match supply with demand.

Monitor Institute estimates the entire impact investment market to be a mere 1 percent of all managed assets by 2020.[17] If only one cent in each investment dollar is likely to be allocated for positive social impact, what impact are the other ninety-nine cents in the investment dollar contributing? The definitional expansion of impact investing should effectively recognize that investment is, in fact, "positively influencing the allocation of capital."[18] Never have truer words been spoken than: "finance is about matching ideas with capital, and capital with great ideas."[19] This idea represents a game-changing opportunity with regard to the other ninety-nine cents in the investment dollar, giving forward-thinking asset managers the chance to enter the impact investment market.

In order for the market to reach its full potential, both in terms of size and scale, there needs to be a robust debate within the finance industry about the role investment plays in society. Since the global financial crisis, the finance industry has been perceived with distrust and negativity, resulting in skepticism toward those in finance. At what point does the finance industry seek to lead by example, or else allow enemies of the industry to define its reason for being? Free markets are the greatest force for good the world has ever seen. The banking and finance industry has played a pivotal role by facilitating the flow of financial resources that fuel capitalism and globalization. There is such a great story to tell the world about the role of finance, and impact investing provides a fantastic narrative to reframe the paradigm. After all, the finance sector plays a pivotal role, either directly or indirectly, in providing the preconditions for wealth creation and prosperity for the entire world. Impact investing can be the source of inspiration to begin rebuilding trust with the greater public, which has been turned off by the perils of myopic selfishness, excessive greed, and global financial turmoil. Therefore, an understanding of the importance of positively influencing the allocation of capital is the critical bedrock for improving the state of the world through finance.

Impact investing also has the potential to become the segment of the broader finance industry at the forefront of positive change, demonstrating that working in finance is a noble cause.[20] Major growth lies not only in the scale of the impact investing market but—when the link between investment and positive impact is demonstrated—there is a natural convergence of goodwill and positivity toward the finance industry. Impact investing is the area that has the greatest potential for repairing the sullied image of Wall Street and the finance industry, while doing immeasurable good for society as a whole.

As the impact investment market grows, in addition to a larger number of investment professionals devoted to the cause, there will inevitably be a broadening of the definition to encompass the increased flow of investment capital. In order for supply to meet demand, the intentionality of impact investment decision making will need to be addressed internally by the investment community. And intentionality matters, but it is not the sole measure of positive social impact. It is self-righteous for the nascent fringe of the industry to argue that explicitly for-profit investments that unintentionally create positive social impact are not pure impact investments. In fact, unintentionality has the profound effect of demonstrating to skeptical investors and mainstream capital alike that strong financial returns and positive social impact are not mutually exclusive. It also sends a price signal to the broader market that it is much easier to do well and do good than they perhaps first thought.

Signaling to the market is critical because it demonstrates that both the impact investment community and the broader community share interests. This is important because there have been many well-intentioned investment strategies, including socially responsible investing,[21] environmental social governance investing,[22] and ethical investing,[23] that have been premised largely on nonfinancial metrics. These investment strategies are popular with some, but have yet to demonstrate holistically a robust investment thesis from a financial perspective. It is often incorrectly assumed that socially responsible and ethical investments are, in fact, impact investments. Socially responsible investing essentially looks at investments through a negative screening process, eliminating investments based on criteria such as whether they include businesses involved in tobacco or weapons. In a similar vein, sustainable investing seeks to screen investments based on active incorporation of environmental, social, and governance criteria. While these well-intentioned strategies may have a positive social impact, they are not ostensibly impact investments because they are not undertaken with the explicit core thesis of delivering positive financial returns and measurable social impact.

As the most influential source of capital, pension funds have a critical role to play in positively influencing the allocation of capital and making impact investing mainstream. In 2014, U.S. pension funds controlled more than $18 trillion, making these funds the largest pool of capital on earth.[24] According to Deloitte, only 6 percent of pension funds have actually made an impact investment. However, management of 64 percent of pension funds said they "expect" to make an impact investment in the future.[25] Therefore, the greatest challenge for the impact investing community is capturing the gigantic deficit between investment capital earmarked for positive social impact and the actual capital deployed in such investment strategies. Pension funds are not alone in this regard, because the same is true for investment by millennials. In the Deloitte study of millennials' investment trends, respondents ranked "to improve society" as the number-one priority of business.[26] This result marginally trumped "generate profit" as millennials' core focus. The study also outlined that this cohort is poised to inherit an estimated $41 trillion from the baby boomers over the next forty years.[27] Millennials' investment dollars and pension funds both have a phenomenal role to play in the mainstreaming of impact investing, as finance managers seek to match their clients' stated desires with meaningful, intentional action.

In an investment industry where Darwinian survival is based on delivering measurable financial performance, investment strategies that are limited in scope bolster the argument that investing based on nonfinancial criteria does a disservice to the investment community more broadly. Whereas socially responsible and sustainable investing may seek to reduce the investment universe, impact investing expands the investment universe. This is a key differentiating factor, because impact investments target positive financial returns as a core plank of the investment rationale. Therefore, impact investing is a phenomenal growth opportunity for the finance industry and has enormous potential to reshape the world as we know it.

## Cultural Revolution for Wall Street

The impact investing approach will transform the ammunition that enemies of free markets use to attack the industry and wealth creation. Impact investing is a game changer for Wall Street because it revolutionizes the way the finance industry will be perceived. Furthermore, impact investing will redefine the powerful force that is capitalism by demonstrating through action that markets are powered by the ethical philosophy of enlightened self-interest. It also provides the great rebuttal to the distorted way in which capitalism was manipulated in the years before and after the global financial crisis. Impact investing not only delivers financial returns to investors, it generates positive social impact to the rest of society. It will also inspire a new raison d'être for a fresh generation of financiers hungry to make the world a better place to live.

Finance has traditionally attracted the best and brightest young minds. However, the global financial crisis acted as a major disruptive force in the banking and finance graduate recruitment process. Harvard University is renowned the world over as the preeminent training ground for those who want to pursue excellence in their chosen academic or professional field. The *Harvard Crimson's* annual survey found that the number of seniors entering finance and consulting was 47 percent in 2007.[28] In 2012, the *Crimson* survey found that only 8.8 percent of the class were headed to finance. In other words, fewer than one in ten graduates chose a career in finance.[29] This was unsurprising, because graduates were deterred from entering the industry by the public outcry over the fatal consequences of the global financial crisis. The low numbers also proved the enormity of the reputational damage to the entire banking and finance industry in the wake of the global financial crisis. Clearly, if the best and brightest minds are choosing alternative careers, the banking and finance industry will eventually face a talent crisis.

Attracting, recruiting, and retaining the best talent is absolutely critical to the reformation of Wall Street's banking and finance culture. Impact investing is a key part of that journey because it shines the light on the philosophical beauty of finance, enlightened self-interest, and free markets as an unstoppable force for good in the world. It is no surprise that Harvard Business School has led the way in encouraging its students to actively incorporate into their coursework case studies and specific classes relating to social finance and impact investing. According to data from the *Harvard Business School Social Enterprise Initiative*, in the 2005–06 academic year there were 395 students enrolled in social enterprise courses and there were 360 cases and teaching notes produced focusing on social enterprise finance.[30] Following the global financial crisis and the resulting disillusionment of students with careers in finance, it is entirely unsurprising that Harvard Business School saw substantial growth in students' interest in social enterprise finance courses. Specifically, by the 2010–11 academic year there were more than 600 students enrolled in social enterprise courses and in excess of 607 cases and teaching notes produced.[31] Course enrollment, student participation, and examination of relevant case studies have had a tremendous impact on students shining the light on this previously misunderstood sector of the finance industry.[32] Impact investing is just the tip of iceberg in terms of reframing the cultural context of banking and finance.

There is little doubt that these graduates will have a unique understanding of the immense power of financial capital to deliver positive social impact and generate profit. This is also a golden opportunity for investment firms to recruit the best talent by promoting their impact investing capabilities as a virtue rather than as a nascent or fringe business unit. As millennials who share a keen sense of communal responsibility and a desire to improve the state of the world populate the workforce, and the finance industry specifically, they will deploy their newfound knowledge, experiences, and talents accordingly. This is just one way the finance industry is being driven from the bottom up to positively influence the allocation of capital and make money by doing good. Impact investing is a key part of the cultural revolution that is taking place in the money management business. If we can change the culture in finance, we can change the world.[33] It is that simple.

## The Role of Millennials

Impact investing is the recalibration of the moral and ethical compass for Wall Street and the finance industry toward true north. The process has begun and it is unstoppable. The millennial generation is driving the impact investing phenomenon from the bottom up because they are eager to make a positive difference, and this trend will have lasting implications. The Deloitte *Millennial Survey 2014* indicated that millennials believe the success of a business should be measured using attributes other than financial performance,[34] and, specifically, should look at improving society as the most important thing business should seek to achieve. According to Deloitte, 74 percent of millennials believe business has an overall positive impact on society, 48 percent believe business improves society by generating jobs, and 71 percent believe business has a positive impact by increasing prosperity.[35] In addition, 50 percent of millennials surveyed expressed a desire to work for a business with ethical practices. Overall, millennials think business can have a positive impact on society.[36]

Millennials have consciously heeded the ethical failures of the past and are therefore more active in public life and civic participation, with 52 percent saying they've signed a petition, indicating a tendency toward political activism.[37] The Deloitte study indicated that 43 percent of millennials volunteer or participate as members of a community organization, while 63 percent of millennials donate money to charities.[38] Millennials believe government is not doing enough to address the greatest societal challenges, and therefore the role of business in making positive impact is deemed even more critical.

Millennials care deeply about the state of the world and the role of business and society, and impact investing is the vehicle they have chosen to embrace as a means by which the private sector can have a positive social impact. Millennials say that they want to work for corporations that are entrepreneurial, and 78 percent are influenced in their career decisions by a company's level of innovation.[39] However, 63 percent of millennials believe that the biggest barrier to innovation is the attitude of old management.[40] Corporations must, therefore, foster innovative thinking in order to embrace millennial leaders as they develop, because 75 percent of millennials believe their organization could do more to develop future leaders.[41] The role of millennials in driving the impact investing movement will only grow more vociferous, credible, and robust as the millennial generation continues to age and grow in size as a demographic cohort. As millennials increase their share of national wealth and become corporate leaders, their ethical values and philosophies will shape their actions.

Impact investing will become the dominant theme sweeping through corporate America and the investment community, whether the current corporate leadership or investment community agrees with it or not. It is here to stay because the tipping point has been reached, and the belief that business and investment have a much greater role to play in society has been accepted. Millennials are driving this ethical perspective, and it is slowly permeating the corporate and investment thought process. Impact investing will only gather pace and scale with time, in large part driven by millennials as they become more demographically relevant and have greater access to financial resources. At that point, a cultural revolution may have completely swept through Wall Street and the finance industry, with firms actively considering positive social impact equally with financial returns. Therefore, impact investing needs to attract the vast swathes of mainstream investment capital and unlock equity markets to have the greatest positive impact.

## Impact Investing and Mainstream Capital

According to the Towers Watson *Global Pension Assets Study*, there were over $18 trillion in pension fund assets in the United States and $31.9 trillion in pension fund assets globally in 2014.[42] If investors positively influence the allocation of capital, this money will leave an indelible mark on the planet by doing immeasurable good for society along the way. It is clear there is a massive market for services that can match the $3.07 trillion[43] of assets under management earmarked for impact investments with robust investment products that meet the needs of investors by delivering superior financial returns and positive social impact. This can be done by mobilizing the hundreds of millions of retail pension fund account holders, many of whom are millennials or other demographic groups, such as women, who care deeply about the world. Democratizing impact investment is the sine qua non for releasing the genie from the bottle. It is just a matter of time before an enlightened individual or firm makes the market and raises several billion dollars.

The fundamental premise of all investment is sustainability. Put simply, successful investments tend to generate additional investment. Likewise, investments that don't preserve capital or that fail to deliver positive returns tend to lower the propensity for further investment. Therefore, any investment strategy, however well intentioned, needs to deliver positive returns in order to survive. Impact investing has the ability to become a sustainable, long-term, and profitable investment strategy if it is given the right industry leadership. Ultimately, this leadership is driven from the top down and the bottom up.

Many institutional investors are actively seeking investment managers who will build a separately managed portfolio that excludes companies based on the arbitrary values and preferences of the investor. This is not impact investing. In order for impact investing to reach its full potential as an investment approach, the retail investor capital pool needs to participate. Once the floodgates are open, the trillions of dollars of retail investor capital will flow freely, and then impact investing will be considered a truly mainstream approach. It is therefore crucial that investors build a strategy to thoroughly articulate how impact investing can be deeply incorporated within a portfolio.

At a macro level, there is clearly a willingness for large pools of capital to be deployed for profit and positive social impact. There is legitimate debate about the authenticity of the asset managers who have signed up to progressive investment principles, such as the United Nations Principles for Responsible Investment, but have yet to make meaningful investment commitments that match their words. The same is true for the impact investing market, where the trillion-dollar opportunity will only be realized when these large pools of capital, including pension funds, endowments, and sovereign wealth funds, are committed in the billions rather than millions. Ultimately, there will come a time when the guardians of asset management firms will be held accountable by their shareholders, pension plan members, voters (in the case of sovereign wealth funds), or militant students (in the case of university endowment funds). When these same guardians sign up to investment principles based on noneconomic factors like negative screening for tobacco, they can be constrained in their investment decision making, and investment returns may thus be penalized.

Furthermore, the premise of arbitrarily restricting investments based on noneconomic factors has an effect opposite to the one intended because it restricts the ability of shareholder capital to influence a company at board level due to investment boycott or blacklisting. It also restricts the investment universe and tends to suppress investment returns, effectively penalizing the investor. Not only does this defeat the purpose of investing, it deters existing and new investors from supporting that investment strategy, however well intentioned.

At the micro level, investors are becoming far savvier in their awareness that the culture in finance needs to reflect changing societal attitudes that value positive social impact alongside financial returns. Smart investors are recognizing the trend and focusing their investment expertise along the dual track of making money and doing good. This seismic shift has the potential to deliver a much-needed cultural revolution in the banking and finance industry, thereby actively rewarding profit that delivers positive social outcomes.

It is clear that the private sector can more effectively solve public policy challenges than the government, and firms that recognize this paradigm shift will likely generate superior financial returns and deliver sizeable positive social impact along the way. Such dual performance will result in greater customer loyalty, sustainability of profits, more favorable publicity, and likely superior shareholder returns over the long term. In the case of Starbucks, the stock price has quadrupled over the six-year period in which the company decided to reduce water consumption by 25 percent.[44]

This further demonstrates that there are rewards for those who are genuine in their pursuit of achieving profit with purpose. As with any investment approach, it is imperative to understand the investment risk and return profiles. For impact investing, the added dimension includes measuring the respective impact risk and return profiles as well. This is true at both the investment and portfolio levels, and is fundamentally important when making rational investment decisions and appropriately monitoring impact investment portfolios. Impact investing will have its day in the sun when investors can no longer justify the opportunity cost between an investment's ability to generate positive social impact and its ability to generate positive risk-adjusted financial returns.

Profit underwrites all future business and investment activities. This indispensable condition is the key to sustainability and continuity for any investment strategy. In terms of impact investing, it is truly remarkable that positive social impact is measured and actively pursued by profit-seeking investment managers. It is important to appreciate the tremendous positive social impact that profit generates, in and of itself. Profitable investments tend to create employment, enabling people to gain self-esteem and meaningful livelihood. This in turn has a multiplier effect in the form of further consumption and investment that delivers tax revenues to governments. At the investment level, profit results in dividends and capital gains to risk-taking owners. In turn, they invest their gains in other productive areas in the form of consumption and investment. This creates a virtuous cycle in which positive social impact creates more positive social impact, empowered by profits. Perhaps it should be called *double-impact investing?* This is just one of the reasons that finance is a force for good.

# Chapter 5

# The Case for Impact: 6E Paradigm

In the decades leading up to the global financial crisis, mainstream investing tended to feature scant regard for an investment's social impact. Warren Buffett, considered by some to be the world's greatest investor, in 2012 told the Forbes 400 Summit, "I think it's tough to serve two masters,"[1] meaning that investors should be skeptical of impact investing that distorts management focus. Moreover, mainstream investing focused almost exclusively on generating profit and shareholder returns. Over time, the neglect of social impact measurement resulted in adverse outcomes that arose from poor investment and resource allocation decisions, as we witnessed in the lead-up to the global financial crisis. The crisis demonstrated the broad-ranging effects of negatively influencing the allocation of capital and focusing ruthlessly on generating short-term profit with scant regard for sustainability and social impact. It also showed conclusively that investments do indeed have impact, and that it is important to measure the impact before it is too late.

There is a perception that impact investments are limited to sophisticated debt instruments, called "pay for success" or social impact bonds, available only to a select group of wealthy family offices and philanthropic foundations. Indeed, in January 2014 the state of Massachusetts announced the largest individual social impact bond ever financed in the United States, a $27 million project designed to reduce recidivism.[2] Deals such as this are encouraging at one level but disappointing at another, because impact investing, and investing in social impact bonds in particular, is easier to talk about than it is to execute. Such projects require an immense level of cooperation between the public and private sectors, and deals can often take years to complete. At the SoCap Conference in 2011, speaker Antony Bugg-Levine, coauthor of *Impact Investing: Transforming How We Make Money While Making a Difference,*[3] said, "I suspect in the history of social innovation there has never been a new product with as high a ratio of words discussed to deals done."[4] Indeed, these kinds of investments are restricted in terms of their liquidity and asset class, making them impossible if not unattractive for the retail investing public to participate in and profit from.

Measurement of impact investment has traditionally focused on the environmental impact of a firm's corporate behavior, sometimes implying a two-dimensional trade-off between profit and environmental impact. This may be because measuring environmental impact is relatively straightforward. This binary outlook is flawed, however, because it fails to consider the full impact of investment across a range of other metrics that are equally important in assessing social impact. In addition, this narrow form of measurement is another reason that impact investing has been unable to gain the prominence it deserves. As a result, impact investing has failed to attract trillions of dollars of institutional investment capital available in the market. According to the Towers Watson *Global Pension Assets Study 2014,* there are $31.9 trillion in global pension fund assets.[5] At the current levels, approximately one-tenth of 1 percent of global pension fund assets are allocated to impact investments. Therefore, in order to attract the trillions of dollars of mainstream investment capital earmarked for achieving positive social impact, there needs to be an alternative approach to making, analyzing, and measuring impact investments.

## Every Investment Has an Impact

Since the global financial crisis, much of the public political and social debate in the investment community has focused on the various global economic imbalances that have either impeded, distorted, or threatened growth. Specifically, such costs have negative social impacts, including deteriorating international relations, political insecurity, and regional conflicts that are enormously threatening to economic prosperity. Not all of these risks are fully priced in an investment, and therefore investment returns are not necessarily correlated with their social impact. Many of these hidden investment risks are due to the failure to account for, and accurately price, the economic costs of the negative externalities. In economic terms, an externality is a cost or benefit of a decision made by one party that affects another party that did not choose to incur that cost or benefit.

Externalities are often blamed for the perception that markets fail, and therefore are used as a justification for government intervention in the free market. From an economic perspective, some externalities are not worth correcting because the benefits of the positive externalities and the costs of the negative externalities effectively cancel each other out. Intervention to correct or regulate a problem can often create larger, unintended consequences, thus amplifying the original problem. For example, airplanes make considerable noise as they descend near an airport, creating a negative externality in the immediate vicinity. Remediating this negative externality, the noise pollution, may involve the government taxing the airline for the noise level, imposing a curfew, or cancelling flights. However, this market intervention imposes far greater costs on the broader economy than the initial negative externality itself, by denying the considerable economic benefits of transport, consumer trade, business, and tourism. Therefore, economists measure externalities according to a consumer's willingness to pay, and this is where government has seized upon an opportunity to collect economic rents in the form of taxation or levies previously valued essentially as free by the private sector. For instance, corporations that pollute the air have previously done so for free but now greater environmental regulations are imposing taxes and charges on carbon released in the atmosphere.

That being said, the major economic and social imbalances between the largest developed and developing nations, vis-à-vis the United States and China, have resulted in negative economic externalities on a much grander scale. Since 1990, structural economic imbalances caused by the meteoric economic rise of China have resulted in tectonic global shifts in the United States and Europe. In 1990, China accounted for 2.30 percent of world's gross domestic product, but had grown to 15.80 percent by 2013 on a purchasing power parity basis.[6] This phenomenal growth in global wealth market share has largely been at the expense of the aggregate European economic community, which saw its share decline from 28.46 percent in 1990 to 18.73 percent in 2013, but also of the United States, where global wealth market share has declined from 24.68 percent in 1990 to 18.62 percent in 2013.[7] China's rise has been fuelled by vast pools of labor that is cheaper than it is in developed economies, sustaining a major global manufacturing hub that exports cheap electronic, household, and fast-moving consumer goods to wealthy customers in the E.U. and the U.S. China has effectively been exporting deflation to the developed world for a quarter century, resulting in the accumulation of major global economic imbalances that threaten the dominance of the United States.

Free trade means that global competition has enhanced the quality of products and reduced prices for consumers across the world, raising their standard of living. Private-sector firms in the developed world rightly argue that they must compete in a global marketplace on an uneven playing field, due to domestic regulations relating to minimum wages, environmental standards, and legal requirements that do not burden companies in developing economies. Private-sector companies in the developed world are burdened with greater costs than their developing world competitors must pay. Therefore, pricing externalities is difficult to achieve unless there is an effective mechanism treating all market participants equally across different geographic jurisdictions.

In the global marketplace, there is no longer an ability to impose trade barriers, because of international free trade agreements enforced by signatories to the World Trade Organization. At this juncture in history, the main threats to prosperity are the huge, uncontained economic imbalances that require international economic cooperation to manage effectively. The most powerful impediment to economic growth and recovery is actually a loss of faith and confidence in the systems that govern established world order. Therefore, attempts by governments in developed economies to strategically price negative externalities domestically while operating in a global marketplace have had unintended, though no less global, ramifications. Impact is felt across the globe with a far-reaching, redistributive wealth effect. Perhaps the attempts were intended to realign the economic imbalances between developed and developing countries that have manifested over the last quarter century.

Governments in the developed world are facing the prospect of sustained economic decline largely as a result of their own policy failures. Suboptimal political behavior and political gridlock stifling economic reform have justified excessive market intervention since the global financial crisis because there is a perception that externalities are widespread, ubiquitous, and cost-free to consumers. However, it was government regulatory policy failure that resulted in the current status quo, whereby the cost of producing externalities is essentially free to the private sector and paid for by society. As a result, economic policy failures have been borne out by a globally orchestrated political campaign among developed economies, including increased deficit and debt accumulation, resulting in catastrophic economic consequences since the global financial crisis and in greater inequality. The majority of governments in the developed economies are capital constrained due to profligate spending, resulting in significant public debt. The policy response to the crisis and the largely ineffective market interventions have laid the foundation for the resulting subdued economic activity.

Below-trend economic growth has restricted governments, politically speaking, in the most industrialized nations from raising income taxes too aggressively in a weak economy. However, public debt–laden governments are desperately searching for alternate methods of revenue generation. Therefore, pricing negative externalities is a means of inventing economic rents that didn't previously exist. In other words, governments are perpetuating the notion that private-sector firms have been free riding in their profit-seeking business activities, creating adverse consequences for society, and should be taxed for those activities. Governments are substantially increasing regulations on private-sector firms with the imposition of additional costs and surrogate taxes relating to perceived negative externalities. Whether this is justified or not is irrelevant because externalities caused in areas like the environment, labor market, and supply chains are being taxed by additional regulatory compliance costs that are ultimately passed on by firms to consumers. In effect, these become an invisible tax increase on consumers via the delivery mechanism of business. Over time, these externalities and regulatory costs will be priced and become a factor in investment decision making. Pricing externalities is one method of dealing with the issue of measuring investment impact and this is an area that investors in developed economies will need to take seriously and factor in, because no corporation is immune to it. Therefore, it stands to reason that forward-thinking investors will be more proactive in terms of recognizing the economic imperative to measure social impact.

## Traditional Impact Measurement: Too Narrow and Two-Dimensional

Impact investing encompasses much more than merely assessing the environmental footprint of capital allocation or an investment. In the past, measuring impact investments has focused mainly on pricing environmental externalities, often as a justification for government regulation. Human achievement over centuries has been empowered by industrial development, which required energy to progress to where the economy is today. Much of the industrialized world's economic development can be traced to its access to reliable and cheap energy. Many of the energy-intensive activities that helped build developed economies would not pass investment filters today, including the building of new coal-fired power plants.

Unfortunately, there is too much simplistic analysis of the perceived trade-off between profits and environmental impact. In order for the impact investing market to grow, there needs to be a more mature outlook, whereby profits are measured against risk-adjusted environmental impact. There are private-sector firms that are doing wonderful things for the environment but are being unfairly penalized by the market because they happen to be in energy-intensive industries. After all, some firms in energy-intensive industries are doing more for sustainability than many firms in relatively low-energy-use industries. Therefore, companies working to reduce their energy use should be congratulated for taking steps to reduce their environmental footprint.

The world's largest mining company is BHP Billiton, and it has been one of the most profitable companies in the world over the last decade. In fact, between 2004 and 2014 BHP Billiton lifted its revenue by 170 percent and its net profit by 294 percent.[8] However, it is less well known that BHP Billiton has also been a market leader in terms of environmental sustainability during that same period. Specifically, BHP Billiton's environmental intensity fell significantly, with a 13 percent reduction in carbon dioxide emissions.[9] In addition, BHP Billiton had only a 5 percent increase in energy and 7 percent increase in water usage during that period.[10] In September 2014, the *Sydney Morning Herald* published an article proclaiming, "BHP is not only leaner, it's greener," to the surprise of many readers who were unaware that the world's largest mining company was so conscious of environmental sustainability.[11] How many other firms in traditional industries like financial services, manufacturing, or retail can boast the same phenomenal record of sustainable environmental and profit achievement over the past decade? The point is that the argument that energy-intensive industries aren't interested in sustainability issues needs to be reframed because, increasingly, environmental footprint is not the optimal measure of the holistic impact of an investment.

Pricing other externalities that government is increasingly regulating, such as labor market conditions, ethical behavior, and education results in hidden costs that are passed on to the private sector by stealth. It is therefore critical for impact investors to accurately measure these economic costs when assessing risk and return expectation. There are various other permutations and constraints that must be accounted for in order to accurately assess, measure, and commit financial resources and maximize positive social impact. If the impact investing community does not look beyond the trade-off between profit and environment, the industry will remain small and largely irrelevant to mainstream global investors, who will be unable to commit investment capital because of rigid impact measurement constraints. In addition, mainstream investors may have genuine intention to allocate investment capital in a way that delivers profit and positive social impact, but may be constrained by the amount of capital, the asset class, or the investment strategy. Therefore, attracting mainstream investment capital requires a new approach to analyzing, measuring, and making impact investments that accurately reflect the full range of social impacts and investment externalities.

## Game Changer: The 6E Paradigm Impact Investing Approach

The 6E Paradigm is a proprietary framework and impact investment strategy that takes a hexagonal approach to measuring profit and social impact. It is intended to complement the financial analysis of an investment by measuring impact holistically, across a range of measures and externalities. The 6E Paradigm is therefore an investment framework that increases both transparency and objectivity while elevating investor confidence in the marketplace and reflecting the true impact of an investment. This tool measures impact as robustly as it measures profit by providing mainstream investors with a framework with which to make impact investments at scale across their entire investment portfolio. The 6E Paradigm is tailored for public equity and stock market investments, but the investment approach can be applied to private equity and debt investments also.

Impact investing is a multitrillion-dollar market opportunity that presents fruits that are ripe for picking. The global rivers of mainstream investment capital will only flow when new sources of capital are encouraged that their investment is actually delivering holistic impact in a transparent manner. When public equity and stock markets are robustly opened up to impact investing, the game changes forever. The 6E Paradigm provides a unique framework for approaching impact investing that enables mainstream investors of any risk profile to positively influence the allocation of capital and appreciate the full impact of investing. It opens up public equity and the stock market to consideration as impact investments by providing a framework that mainstream investors can use to measure impact.

## The Theory Behind the 6E Paradigm

The 6E Paradigm is a framework that objectively considers data and metrics relating to the impacts of the six Es of an investment: economics, employment, empowerment, education, ethics, and environments.

### 1. Economics

***Economics is concerned with calculating the value of the company share price.*** The majority of investors tend to evaluate stock prices based exclusively on the economics or financials of a company by looking at quantitative measures for a valuation. If an investor predicts that the valuation will be higher in the future than the current price reflects, the investor will buy the stock. Conversely, if an investor expects the valuation to be lower in the future than the current price, the investor will choose not to buy the stock. Investors have various theoretical viewpoints in terms of calculating the value of a stock. As risk increases, the investor's required rate of return increases to compensate for the additional risk.

There are two basic approaches to stock price analysis: fundamental and technical. Fundamental analysis is applied to determine the intrinsic value of the stock by projecting future earnings and then applying an acceptable return on investment to calculate the stock price. This is a traditional investment approach and forms the basis for stock price valuation. Fundamental analysis essentially calculates what a stock price *should* be in the future. In contrast, technical analysis applies statistical techniques to historical stock prices and volumes to identify future price movements, giving no consideration to the fundamentals of the company. Stock price data incorporates price movements driven by human behavior, thus differentiating technical and fundamental analysis. At any point in time, investment stock price analysis requires an appreciation of both the fundamental and technical elements to effectively determine a valuation.

## 2. Employment

***Employment is concerned with direct and indirect job creation.*** Investment performs a critical role in the infusion of capital to fund productive businesses that create vital employment and deliver profit. Successful firms tend to employ more people, in contrast with less successful firms that view employees as tradable commodities. In 1914, American industrialist Henry Ford decided to double workers' pay and raise wages to $5 per day at his Ford Motor Company. He argued that, "We were building for the future. A low-wage business is always insecure."[12] With one stroke of his executive pen, Henry Ford would shape corporate America and leave a template for generations about the importance of paying a decent wage. Needless to say, increasing wages proved extremely profitable at Ford Motor Company because it allowed the company to attract the best-trained staff, reduce employee turnover, and increase productivity. This single action demonstrated the importance of employment as a critical function, and included employees as vital partners in a successful business. As the United States industrialized over the next three decades, labor relations would perform an integral role in shaping the way the economy developed.

During the half-century after the end of World War II, flows of people internationally closely followed economic growth patterns. In the post-war immigration boom, millions of people relocated from less wealthy parts of Asia, Eastern Europe, and Africa to seek opportunities for a better life in larger industrializing countries, including the relatively affluent United States, United Kingdom, and Australia. In other words, labor followed capital. However, the reverse occurred in the quarter century leading up to the global financial crisis, and capital followed labor. Labor costs in the developing world were significantly cheaper than in large economies like the U.S., which has minimum wage laws, powerful trade unions, and labor regulations that raise the cost of employment.

Countries like China, Bangladesh, Vietnam, and Indonesia were largely unburdened by such labor restraints and were more than accommodating to Western firms seeking to outsource manufacturing jobs to the large, unregulated, and cheaper pools of efficient labor. Over the past quarter century, the global economy grew in both the East and West, though ruthless global competition would see a race to the bottom in terms of reducing manufacturing and labor costs. This had dramatic consequences for the living standards and quality of life for people in the developed economies, who tended to buy more and save less while people in the developing countries tended to buy less and save more. This phenomenon played a major role in the mounting economic imbalances between the developing and developed world that accumulated over time in the lead-up to the global financial crisis. In the aftermath of the financial crisis, governments in the developed economies were under greater pressure to increase domestic employment and economic growth. When the economy ground to a halt in the U.S. in 2008, local jobs were scarce and there was also a growing political backlash against large firms hiring foreign workers at the expense of unemployed Americans.

In a modern, industrialized, market-based economy, government is manifestly incapable of being a major employer. In fact, government policies in response to the global financial crisis have demonstrated that it is the private sector that is best equipped to drive sustainable economic growth. It is the private sector that is at the heart of generating wealth creation and employment. Impact investors ought to be cognizant of the role they play in the vital area of employment by allocating capital toward companies and businesses. In a stagnant global economy with record youth unemployment, investments should account for their impact on employment.

Businesses that grow their labor force, share profits with employees, and incentivize productivity tend to be better corporate citizens, demonstrating the power of the private sector in delivering positive social impact.

The benefits of technology and innovation include an increase in higher-skilled, higher-paying employment across the economy. Employment creates more employment, increases economic activity, and raises tax revenues. Growth of the trust economy has had a great impact on entrepreneurial employment opportunities, with secondary and tertiary employment required to service the higher-skilled jobs, including hospitality, medical, and banking jobs. Research by labor economist Enrico Moretti, a professor at the University of California, Berkeley, suggests that sixty thousand additional services jobs were created as a result of Apple Corporation having twelve thousand employees in Cupertino, California.[13] Investment in businesses that create employment will have vastly greater impact than investment in businesses that don't. Such employment metrics are crucial for investors to fully understand the depth and breadth of their investment, as well as the multiplier effect that finance can have in the economy. Firms that hire more people by generating additional direct and indirect employment are delivering positive social impact and should be recognized as impact investments.

## 3. Empowerment

***Empowerment is concerned with the robust diversity of company stakeholders.*** Company executives have a huge role to play in terms of delivering a positive impact for their stakeholders, including employees, shareholders, and the community. Business fulfills an incredibly important leadership role, and company leaders are the primary driver of this endeavor. Corporate values are the seeds planted by leadership that determine the business culture.

Incentives set by company leadership ultimately shape the business culture. Behavior is therefore the product of the business culture, and is often modeled on the business leadership. Corporate behavior then drives the business outcomes. If any step along the process is flawed or suboptimal, it is likely that the leadership has direct or indirect responsibility. Impact measurement must therefore also include the degree to which a company, and its leadership, empowers its stakeholders to amplify their corporate purpose.

Racial and ethnic diversity, as well as a more even balance of male and female executives, is a key component to executive leadership and has a substantial role to play in terms of decision making and financial performance. Before the global financial crisis, there was scant emphasis on the importance of diversity and the role of confirmation bias in decision making. The case for increased diversity, particularly in banking and financial services, is that leadership of the major investment banks in the lead-up to the global financial crisis appeared strikingly similar: the chief executives were overwhelmingly male, Caucasian, and Ivy League educated.[14] Proponents of increased diversity argue that relying on a specific talent pool constrains the success of an organization and its ability to generate innovative ideas. Increasing diversity in terms of experience, background, gender, nationality, and thought process is a critical component for companies to consider given the global marketplace in which they operate. Indeed, there has been much criticism that the finance industry lacks robust diversity, underscored by the perception of a male-dominated culture that is glamorized by films such as Martin Scorsese's *The Wolf of Wall Street*.[15]

Increased diversity has a critical role to play in the continued evolution of the finance industry. According to *New York Magazine's* Kevin Roose, "Almost every major bank has been sued for gender discrimination at some point."[16] Clearly, rectifying the unhealthy stereotypes requires brave internal leadership, or else outside parties will intervene. In response to the global financial crisis, the Dodd–Frank Wall Street Reform and Consumer Protection Act was signed into law on July 21, 2010, in the U.S. The act directed financial regulators to propose new standards for a system to monitor diversity practices at banks and established the Office of Minority and Women Inclusion.[17] It is indeed disappointing that the banking industry requires government intervention to promote increased diversity. Greater diversity and inclusion ensures stronger, more effective, and more innovative businesses, which are critical as the financial services sector leads the economic recovery.

There is evidence that increased executive diversity has a positive impact on financial performance by expanding a company's strategic perspective and risk profile. In April 2012, *McKinsey Quarterly* produced an article titled "Is There a Payoff from Top-Team Diversity?" According to the research, McKinsey studied executive board composition of 180 publicly traded companies in the United States, United Kingdom, France, and Germany during the period from 2008 to 2010.[18] The results found that companies ranking in the top quartile of executive board diversity achieved returns on equity 53 percent higher on average than those in the bottom quartile.[19] In addition, companies ranking in the top quartile achieved earnings margins 14 percent higher on average than those in the bottom quartile.[20] These results make a compelling case that greater board diversity has a positive impact on company financial performance.

Businesses should not require government intervention to promote increased diversity, because this effectively becomes another externality for which companies will need to pay. The business case for greater diversity is strong, as companies that promote diversity tend to outperform their competitors. Therefore, executive leadership empowerment is a fundamentally important measure for quantifying an investment's full impact. Empowerment in the form of greater diversity is a healthy indicator of financial performance, resulting in a positive social impact for the society and other stakeholders.

## 4. Education

***Education is concerned with measuring the cost of compliance and continuous improvement of the company.*** Increased government regulation has resulted in compliance becoming a significant business cost. Internal compliance requirements are actions that must be taken by stakeholders to ensure that good corporate governance measures are followed. Corporations have strict internal compliance requirements, including holding annual shareholder and director meetings, maintaining robust financial records, and implementing security measures. External compliance costs include annual and quarterly reporting, legal and accounting fees, and continuous disclosure requirements. Failure to comply with regulations can be very expensive for a corporation and may result in severe sanctions. Therefore, firms are required to educate and train staff with appropriate accreditation to perform specific duties. For instance, the Securities and Exchange Commission requires an individual who seeks to enter the securities industry to take the Series 7 examination.

The Financial Industry Regulatory Authority administers the Series 7 examination in addition to other compliance requirements ranging from Series 3 to Series 99.[21] Raising the standards of professional accreditation is an important step in the continuous improvement of the banking and finance industry in the aftermath of the global financial crisis. Similarly, the increased compliance burden results in the increase in ongoing education costs associated with professional development. Firms that recognize the importance of proactive continuous improvement will realize the dividend of a more productive and highly educated workforce. This, in turn, is likely to reduce the probability of ethical malpractice or professional negligence. In addition, a workforce that has greater professional development and training enhances the overall education level of the industry.

Corporations have a great role to play in terms of promoting increased educational attainment among employees. The multiplier effect across society is felt far beyond the workplace as people increase their knowledge, skills, and accreditation. Highly skilled knowledge workers are more likely to earn higher incomes; according to the Pew Research Center, 49.7 percent of aggregate household income in 2012 went to households headed by someone with at least a bachelor's degree.[22] Education has additional benefits for society at large, because higher incomes result in greater tax revenues. Higher education levels also reduce the likelihood of poverty and improve health outcomes. As society lifts general education levels, the entire population benefits with lower rates of poverty. This is a critical role for the private sector to consider because education is a public good that they can deliver, thus reducing reliability on the government and enabling public resources to be allocated more efficiently. This enables scarce public resources to be allocated more effectively to meet the greatest public need.

Investments that fund companies that increase the skill and knowledge base of their workforce benefit society to a much greater extent than investments that do not. Technology has increased the skill and knowledge base of millions of workers by increasing their efficiency, accuracy, and productivity. Business has a far greater function in facilitating the expansion of knowledge and skills than ever before. Companies that recognize this opportunity will benefit tremendously by investing in the best talent and being the most profitable. Therefore, understanding the full impact of investment requires a thorough appreciation of the pivotal role that education plays in society. Corporations that leverage this capability are infinitely more impactful. Impact investors should therefore measure the educational footprint of their investments when assessing total impact.

## 5. Ethics

***Ethics are concerned with the moral principles that govern the company's behavior.*** Ethical judgments guide humans to make a choice between right and wrong. Corporations are made up of people, and the executives who lead are responsible for enacting and implementing the company's guidelines for behavior. In business, transactions are formed on the basis of trust and commercial credibility. Executives are the custodians of corporate reputation, and this element must be reviewed repeatedly to ensure that behavior follows values. Measuring ethical behavior is a difficult but critical task, as the impact of unethical behavior can result in major systemic failure. Indeed, failure to appropriately value ethics can prove extremely costly. Corporations play such a large role in everyday life that their actions are not confined to the boardroom, but rather have widespread ramifications. Understanding the true impact of investing, and appropriately analyzing investment impact, requires a proper appraisal of the ethics and principles guiding the executives leading the firm.

Ethical behavior tends to be modeled from the top of an organization. Firms led by executives focused ruthlessly on short-term profit will be motivated by greed rather than by long-term business success. Incentives play an important role in guiding the ethical behavior of corporate executives, and alignment of interests is therefore an important factor in calculating incentives. Executive compensation provides a unique indicator in this regard, and can in some sense measure the degree to which ethics are valued in an organization. Firms that incentivize executives by offering a greater share of their compensation based on long-term equity are more likely to be interested in the long-term success of the firm. Therefore, executive compensation is a critical component in assessing the ethical balance of a corporation and the probability of success over the long term.

Success is the antithesis of failure. Corporate failure is often linked to, and the direct result of, egregious ethics violations. Some of the most notable corporate failures have led to billions of dollars in shareholder value destruction. The corporate failure and bankruptcy of Enron Corporation in 2001, for example, serves as a cautionary tale and underlines the importance of company executives who act with integrity.[23] Enron had a meteoric rise from a small natural gas pipeline company to the seventh-largest publicly held corporation in the United States. Enron's swift rise became a legendary tale of risk-taking entrepreneurship and business success, with fabulous financial rewards shared among the winning executives and shareholders. However, the rise of Enron was met with an equally spectacular fall, as some Enron executives were also guilty of employing suspicious accounting practices and risk management, exploiting loopholes, and using special-purposes vehicles and weak reporting. In so doing, they hid billions of dollars in debts and other losses.[24] Executives also allegedly misled the board, auditors, and the market as to the true state of corporate performance in an attempt to inflate the stock price and enrich themselves. In total, sixteen former Enron executives were convicted and sentenced to prison for their role in the collapse.[25] Enron is a stark reminder that corporate failure is measured not only in loss of shareholder value but in lives destroyed.[26] At its peak, Enron employed close to twenty-two thousand people, and its collapse resulted in greater scrutiny on corporations to improve transparency and corporate governance practices.[27] The collapse of Enron sent reverberations across the corporate world and reinvigorated the idea that strong ethics ought to be a core principle of executives entrusted with fiduciary responsibility.

The global financial crisis demonstrated numerous instances of egregious ethical violations, indicating the importance of accounting for ethical impacts in investments. Perhaps the greatest example of an ethical violation, one that came to symbolize the global financial crisis, was the $65 billion Ponzi scheme run by New York hedge fund manager Bernard L. Madoff.[28] Despite numerous red flags, neither the Securities and Exchange Commission nor investors exposed the duplicitous investment scheme until the mastermind was arrested on December 11, 2008.[29] Thousands of investors lost their entire investment, including a number of nonprofit and philanthropic organizations. This is, of course, the cruelest of ironies, because many of these philanthropic and foundation investors embodied ethical behavior, among them the Elie Wiesel Foundation for Humanity, established by Nobel Laureate Elie Wiesel and his wife, Marion.[30] In the business world, as in life, ethics are often only valued in a time of stress or crisis, by which time they have already been lost.

These scandals have shocked the corporate world and highlighted the vastly important role that ethical judgment and trust play in managing shareholder assets. In 2011, government regulators like the U.S. Securities and Exchange Commission were given new powers to encourage people to come forward with evidence of securities fraud. The new program financially rewards a whistleblower with 10 to 30 percent of the money collected in the case, demonstrating a strong emphasis on insider assistance.[31] Despite deterrence measures that include criminal punishment, a prison sentence, and a heavy financial penalty, there will always be a risk that company executives will be susceptible to ethics violation in the future. Investing in firms that have a robust code of business ethics, share a commitment to corporate social responsibility, and avoid condoning or appearing to condone poor ethical behavior will deliver greater measurable impact than investing in firms that do not. By refusing to allocate capital to unethical companies, investors can positively influence the whole business world: when an unethical firm finds itself with no customers, no suppliers, and no investors, it will be forced to change behavior or will simply go out of business. Therefore, investors that value exemplary ethical behavior are likely to make a greater positive impact with their investments.

## 6. Environment

***Environment is concerned with the company's impact on the planet.*** Impact investing has tended to focus almost exclusively on the environmental impact of an investment. In many respects, environmental impact is perhaps the easiest and most tangible dimension to account for, other than investment return. Measuring an investment's environmental impact is important because it provides a quantifiable measure of investment externalities like air pollution, carbon dioxide emissions, and energy intensity. Measuring such impacts provides valuable data for comparing and contrasting relative information from company to company, industry to industry, and year to year. These objective measures provide valuable information that allows company executives and management, shareholders, and the community to fully understand the environmental impact of their decisions. Importantly, environmental impact and externalities create costs to society in the form of air pollution, waste, and resource depletion. In the case of air pollution from a factory, some of these costs are borne by society at large in terms of reduced air quality. But this may change with increased pressure on government and regulators to make companies pay for pollution. It is no surprise that regulations to curb carbon dioxide emissions have steadily increased over the years. These regulations attempt to pressure private-sector corporations to shift the way they conduct their business, in an effort to minimize environmental impact.

The benefits of incorporating environmental information into business strategy are important because there are costs associated with greater environmental regulation. For instance, firms that recognize the financial incentive to become more energy efficient will be better placed to absorb rising energy costs. Moreover, resource scarcity and subsequent environmental impact are increasingly becoming broader social issues, resulting in a political response of enhanced regulations. Thus, there is a link between sustainability and more stable business conditions, including enhanced community relations and improved resource efficiency, which will generate financial benefits. This is consistent with the findings of a Harvard Business School working paper titled *The Impact of a Corporate Culture of Sustainability on Corporate Behavior and Performance,* released in 2012.[32]

The Harvard Business School study analyzed companies over an eighteen-year period and concluded that high-sustainability companies tended to outperform their low-sustainability competitors.[33] Specifically, the study outlined that companies with high-sustainability performance saw annual market performance that was 4.8 percent higher, and with lower volatility, than that of companies with low-sustainability performance.[34] In addition, companies with high-sustainability performance were found to outperform companies with low-sustainability performance in other metrics, including return on assets and return on equity. Moreover, the study found that the outperformance by high-sustainability companies was more pronounced for firms that sell products directly to individuals and competed on the basis of reputation and brand.[35] The implication is that customers are becoming far more aware of environmental sustainability, and companies that incorporate these values will be rewarded by customers.

The mainstream investment community is becoming more aware of environmental issues after decades of political debate highlighting them. Additionally, nongovernmental organizations, special interest groups, and socially responsible investors have been calling for greater environmental consideration. Governments in developed countries are under increasing pressure by the United Nations to reduce carbon dioxide emissions and encourage corporations to become more environmentally sustainable. Many countries require companies listed on the stock exchange to disclose their environmental impact; among these countries are the United States, Australia, Brazil, Canada, China, India, and South Africa.[36] Firms that are adaptive to the environmental considerations of government, customers, and other stakeholders will outperform their competitors in terms of delivering positive social impact and financial performance.

## Applying the 6E Paradigm to Starbucks Corporation

Starbucks Corporation is the premier marketer, roaster, and retailer of specialty coffee in the world. Commonly referred to as simply Starbucks, the company is recognized as the industry leader in all things coffee. In 2014, Starbucks was the largest coffeehouse company in the world, operating in sixty-five countries and territories with more than twenty-three thousand stores offering more than eighty-seven thousand espresso drink combinations and serving more than ten million cups of coffee per day.[37] Starbucks is led by Howard Schultz, a visionary leader who became chief executive officer in 1987. Schultz's business concerns extend far beyond the corporate bottom line, and he attributes the company's success to a business model that balances profitability and social consciousness, and that places employees and communities at the core. "Starbucks represents something beyond a cup of coffee," Schultz has said.[38] During the period Schultz has led Starbucks, the company share price has grown more than 12,300 percent.[39] A model corporation in terms of balancing profit and social impact, Starbucks has delivered both simultaneously over a long period of time. The company offers an exemplary case study of a publicly listed corporation that ought to be considered an impact investment because it intentionally delivers both measurable positive social impact and strong financial returns.

In 2014, Starbucks' total market capitalization touched $60 billion,[40] roughly equivalent to the total gross domestic product of Luxembourg, one of the wealthiest nations in the world based on per capita income. Starbucks generates close to $16 billion in annual revenue, serving more than three billion customers and using more than four billion paper cups per year.[41] In fact, the company embodies the very essence of enlightened self-interest.

## 1. Economics

In 1992, Starbucks undertook an initial public offering and listed on the NASDAQ, trading under the symbol SBUX. In the two decades since, its stock price has risen more than 12,300 percent,[42] indicating phenomenal outperformance and beating the S&P 500, Dow Jones Industrial Average, Russell 2000, and NASDAQ Composite. During that time period, Starbucks has been incredibly profitable as a company, generating billions of dollars in corporate profits, dividends, and taxes. Howard Schultz has not been a leader to rest on his laurels, rather articulating a core belief that, "Companies should not have a singular view of profitability. There needs to be a balance between commerce and social responsibility. The companies that are authentic about it will wind up as the companies that make more money."[43] Going even further, he said, "Profitability is a shallow goal if it doesn't have a real purpose and the purpose has to be share the profits with others," he said.[44] Starbucks Corporation has been an ideal case study of a company that is delivering significant shareholder performance while delivering great positive social impact around the world.

## 2. Employment

Starbucks is a leader in best-of-class corporate citizenship and employee engagement, with a diverse and inclusive corporate culture that in 2013 included more than two hundred thousand employees.[45] Moreover, Starbucks has been at the forefront of many employee-related issues, including education and health care. Employees are considered "partners," with a range of benefits available depending on hours worked; to be eligible, employees must work more than twenty hours per week. The employee benefits package can include discounted stock options and health coverage for dependents.[46] According to Schultz, "Starbucks is not an advertiser; people think we are a great marketing company, but in fact we spend very little money on marketing and more money on training our people than advertising."[47] Starbucks continues to demonstrate a commitment to the communities they serve by valuing education and employee commitment to community service. In 2012, Starbucks sponsored more than six hundred thousand hours of community service by employees and customers. By 2015, the firm seeks to expand the service commitment to one million hours.[48]

## 3. Empowerment

Starbucks is a leader in empowerment and global diversity, with a workforce in the United States comprising 63 percent women and 24 percent people of color. At the executive level, 32 percent are female and 13 percent are people of color.[49] These figures compare favorably to other Fortune 500 companies, which average an executive pool that is roughly 15 percent female and 3 to 5 percent people of color.[50] Perhaps the most impressive statistics at Starbucks involve the continuing commitment to its Supplier Diversity Program, which tracks spending with minority-owned and women-owned businesses in the supply chain. Spending with these groups has more than doubled, to $140 million, up from $69 million in 2002.[51] Supplier diversity is not only a smart business decision for Starbucks, it builds resilient and prosperous communities as well.

## 4. Education

Starbucks is a leader in empowering its employees and encouraging them toward educational attainment. In 2014, the company launched the Starbucks College Achievement Plan by offering all eligible employees scholarships to attend college online, in partnership with Arizona State University.[52] The Starbucks College Achievement Plan stipulates that employees "will have no commitment to remain at Starbucks past graduation," according to the company.[53] This demonstrates the view that employees enhancing their education benefits Starbucks and society as a whole. Starbucks is creating positive social impact by empowering its employees to reach their potential as professionals, citizens, and human beings.

## 5. Ethics

Starbucks is led by an executive team committed to the highest values and ethical standards across all elements of the business. These values extend beyond the employment function to include other elements of the Starbucks supply chain. The world's leading coffee-exporting countries are developing economies, including Brazil, Vietnam, Indonesia, and Colombia.[54] These countries have less robust institutions, weaker nongovernmental organizations, and lighter government regulation of labor and environmental standards than the United States.

Coffee is a commodity that grows as a berry, which is often

washed and dried out by hand before it is processed and exported thousands of miles by rail and ship. In the past, coffee bean production has been characterized as an opaque agricultural industry with questionable ethical practices, including child labor, deforestation, and poor environmental processes. Starbucks has been an industry leader in the development of the Coffee and Farmer Equity Practices, working closely with Conservation International.[55] The framework is a set of two hundred guiding principles that ensure that social, economic, and environmental sourcing standards are adopted and implemented across the Starbucks global supply chain.[56] In 2013, 95.3 percent of Starbucks coffee was ethically sourced through the Coffee and Farmer Equity Practices, getting closer to the ultimate goal of 100 percent ethically sourced coffee by 2015.[57] Starbucks' ethical standards are having an immensely positive impact on the lives of people across the world as the ethical principles guiding Starbucks extend to all layers of the business, supply chain, stakeholders, and the environment.

## 6. Environment

Starbucks recognizes the important leadership role companies can play in making a positive impact on the environment. As the business continues to grow, Starbucks continues to use more and more paper cups, currently more than four billion per year. In collaboration with stakeholders including government, paper producers, and competitors, Starbucks set a goal to make 100 percent of its cups reusable or recyclable by 2015.[58] This ambitious goal is revolutionary for the global beverage industry and will have a profound environmental impact.

Starbucks has also recognized that another key natural resource is increasingly important to the company and environment. Water is a key ingredient in coffee and is used across the business in activities from cleaning to dishwashing to ice-making. Water is also a key input cost to the business, and Starbucks set a target to reduce water consumption by 25 percent in company-owned stores by 2015.[59] Improved water efficiency, replacement of old equipment, and water-saving techniques implemented on the landscaping of new stores have all contributed to lower water consumption. These innovative methods are having measurable and positive environmental impact as a well as being financially accretive.

## Game Changer: Impact Investing and Unlocking the Stock Market

According to the 6E Paradigm, Starbucks Corporation gets a six-star rating, the highest possible designation. Starbucks is an example of a leading U.S. corporation that is having a greater positive social impact than is often appreciated by the capital markets, investors, stakeholders, and general public. How many investors realize the positive impact they are having by supporting a corporation that has such a deep and interconnected global footprint, and that delivers measurable positive social impact and excess market financial performance? In fact, the firm is having far greater global social impact than many designated impact investments. If other companies listed on the stock market followed Starbucks' leadership, the world would be a vastly different place. This demonstrates the importance of the 6E Paradigm in providing a framework that measures holistic impact: the 6E Paradigm impact investing framework enables all capital allocators, ranging from small retail investors to large-scale sovereign wealth funds, to positively influence their allocation of capital.

The traditional two-dimensional impact investing approach is too narrow because it seeks only to focus on profit and environment. As a result, mainstream investors genuinely seeking to allocate capital for positive social impact without compromising investment returns are constrained by the lack of sufficient robust investment opportunities. This constraint also reduces the asset classes available for making impact investments, reducing the capacity for trillions of dollars in mainstream investment capital to enter the market. After an investor is satisfied with the economics of a particular investment, the 6E Paradigm positively screens the investment's full impact on employment, education, empowerment, ethics, and environment before allocating capital. Therefore, the hexagonal perspective of the 6E Paradigm enables investors to be unbound by arbitrary limitations that restrict their ability to invest in certain assets or to accurately account for the impact of certain investments. This strategic investment approach is applicable to all asset classes, effectively opening up impact investing to an entire portfolio, meaning greater positive social impact and profits delivered with good conscience. There is a distinct first-mover advantage to be gained by asset managers and private-sector firms that factor these externalities into their equations and allocate capital accordingly.

The most significant barrier to entry for impact investing as a mainstream activity has been the inability to effectively analyze public equity and stock market investments, an inability that limits the scale and market that impact investment can develop. The 6E Paradigm as an investment approach is particularly attractive and unique in terms of analyzing stock market and public equity investments. Investment liquidity is the most important feature of investing in the stock market because it uniquely allows investors the ability to enter and exit the market instantaneously. This is the investment approach that can revolutionize the impact investing industry, because effectively opening up the stock market to impact investing is the trillion-dollar genie in the bottle waiting to escape. There is a substantial market inefficiency that will close over the long term, when impact is accurately priced into the investment equation. Investors who factor in the costs of negative externalities imposed on corporations will ultimately prevail over the long term when the market inefficiency is closed.

It is important to understand the theory behind each parameter of the 6E Paradigm and then to recognize its application to fully appreciate how impact investing can, and should, be applied to stock market investing. Thorough analysis using the paradigm can open up the capacity for trillions of dollars of equity investment to flow to firms that deliver profit and positive social impact. Incorporating the hexagonal framework of the 6E Paradigm allows investors to account for the full impact of their investments and it expands the potential impact investment universe.

This investment approach unlocks the constraints facing the majority of mainstream investors: a limited supply of robust impact investment options. The 6E Paradigm enables mainstream investors, particularly equity investors, to positively influence the allocation of capital by analyzing, measuring, and making impact investments in an asset class previously excluded from the mix. For impact investing to become a mainstream investment theme, the equity markets need to be opened up because they are the largest asset class and attract the most capital. Impact investing shouldn't be viewed as foreign to equity investing, but rather as a core component of it. As of September 2014, the total market index was over $21 trillion, equivalent to 124 percent of the gross domestic product of the United States.[60] Once the listed equity market is opened up to the realm of impact investing, the behavior of other firms in a competitive marketplace will change. The rivers of mainstream investment capital will flow, nourishing companies that are intentionally delivering positive social impact and generating solid financial returns.

*That is the impact of investing.*

# Chapter 6

## Finance as a Force for Good

Rather than a stand-alone asset class, impact investing is an investment approach to allocating capital. There are certain asset classes, however, that have a demonstrably greater positive social impact than others that also generate financial returns to investors on a grand scale. Impact investing has the power to transform the entire finance industry, and therefore revolutionize the whole world. In the marketplace every investment has the capacity to deliver positive social impact, and it is important to think about allocating capital accordingly to maximize impact. There is much focus on the nonprofit sector but not nearly as much emphasis on the critical importance of the for-profit sector and the immense positive impact it has, and can have, on society. There are myriad ways mainstream investors can actively re-weight their portfolios toward these assets classes and investment themes, in addition to making bespoke impact investments.

It is important to begin the process of democratizing impact investment vehicles by opening them up to retail investors. In the United States, there are in excess of $18 trillion in pension fund assets, effectively the retirement savings pool of more than one hundred million people. Globally, there are $31.98 trillion in pension fund assets, representing the accounts of more than a billion people.[1] In order for the power of finance to achieve the greatest good for society, impact investment opportunities need to be of a size that can attract billions and then trillions of dollars in financial capital. When impact investing reaches that size and scale, it will have the power to realize optimal benefits for both society and investors.

Positive social impact and financial return need not compete for attention; they can robustly coexist. Positive social impact and financial returns can be further maximized by an alignment of values, incentivizing investors at all risk levels to embrace the impact investing approach. This chapter outlines the opportunities for investors to positively influence the allocation of capital by exploring the most robust impact investment approach consistent with their risk profiles, thus recognizing the breadth of finance to act as a force for good in the world.

## Financial Inclusion

The World Bank estimated that there were 2.5 billion people globally—the majority of them working-age adults—who in 2014 had no access to formal financial services delivered by regulated financial institutions.[2] In a world with a population of 7.125 billion people,[3] that means about 36 percent of the world population is currently outside the formal financial services tent. This segment of the population is effectively *unbanked,* or at best underbanked. In order for finance to reach its greatest potential as a force for good, the vast majority of the world population needs to have financial services available to them. Therefore, financial inclusion is an essential growth area for the entire finance industry, which should lead the way in delivering prosperity to the billions of people at the bottom of the financial pyramid. Financial inclusion involves providing safe financial institutions that are governed by clear and effective regulations and that meet industry performance benchmarks. Financial institutions must be viable, going concerns, ensuring continuity and certainty of investment and providing competition and choice for customers. In addition, financial inclusion means access to a full suite of basic financial services at a reasonable cost, including savings and deposits, payment, funds transfer, insurance, and credit. Formal financial services are preferable to the alternative black market for financial services, which is characterized as informal, opaque, unscrupulous, and unsafe.

In a functioning civil society based on trust and rule of law, banking provides a critical service. The world is a safer place when people can safely store their possessions and financial resources in a secure and stable environment. In a contrarian world, where people have to protect their own financial wealth and money informally, there is greater civil disorder, instability, and crime. It is preferable for all humans to have access to basic financial services that empower them to realize a prosperous existence.

In the developing world, people need financial services such as savings vehicles, insurance, credit, and payments to assist them in managing their lives. Basic financial management provides the stability that allows people to build better a future and sustain their families. However, very few people have access to such services from formal financial service providers. It is estimated that only 24 percent of adults in sub-Saharan Africa have access to a bank account. Moreover, the World Bank estimates that three quarters of the world's poor do not have a bank account at all, due not only to poverty but to the paperwork and costs involved.[4] This is despite the fact that the formal financial services sector in Africa has grown in recent years.

The importance of financial inclusion in curbing illicit money flows cannot be understated. Global Financial Integrity, a nonprofit research and advisory organization, reported that illicit financial outflows from developing world economies were $946.7 billion in 2011, and cumulative outflows reached a staggering $5.9

trillion between 2002 and 2011.[5] This data gives further evidence to the fact that illicit financial flows, a euphemism for corruption and kleptocracy, are the most devastating economic issue adversely impacting economies in the developing world. In other words, twenty African countries have lost the equivalent of 10 percent of their gross domestic product every year since 1980 due to illicit financial outflows. Some of the illicit funds are the result of kleptocracy and corruption, while other funds derive from old-fashioned money-laundering schemes in which individuals or companies over-invoice, altering the value of their imports and exports. This enables unscrupulous individuals to move money between jurisdictions illegally.[6] Illicit financial flows must be addressed in order for economic development to broaden and benefit the most vulnerable people at the bottom of the economic pyramid. Financial inclusion must therefore make basic banking and payment services available to the entire population of Africa, in addition to curbing corruption. There is a clear correlation between high-touch financial inclusion and a stable financial system that promotes broad economic growth and participation.

Significant advances in technology and access to information and data will no doubt play a key role in facilitating greater financial inclusion in the coming decade. Financial services are clearly a growth area in terms of technological integration driving enhanced access and inclusion in the financial system. Technology has enhanced the financial services offerings, made them more accessible, increased competition, and made services more affordable to consumers across the developing world. Already there have been successes in recent years, with the proportion of people in Tanzania excluded from formal financial services falling from 70 percent to 50 percent of the population. In Nigeria, the proportion of the population excluded from financial services has dropped from 47 percent to 39 percent. This is important evidence demonstrating that financial inclusion is achievable and successful when advancing technology is incorporated into the strategy. Access to financial services is accelerating due to the scope of the business opportunity for firms in the developed world seeking growth opportunities in emerging and frontier markets.

In the developing world, microfinance has traditionally been the sole source of financial services and private capital for entrepreneurs and small business owners who lack access to mainstream banking services. Microfinance has tended to be relationship-based, with either individual entrepreneurs or a group applying for small loans to launch a business servicing their community. Bangladeshi economist Muhammad Yunus, regarded as the father of microfinance,[7] in 1983 formally launched Grameen Bank, which mainly services women who want to establish small businesses. According to Grameen, 97 percent of its customers are women and there is a 98 percent repayment rate. According to the World Bank, where women have access to microfinance and microcredit, they have greater access to resources and more control over economic decision making within their families, leading to higher productivity and economic development. In 2006, Muhammad Yunus and Grameen Bank were jointly awarded the Nobel Peace Prize "for their efforts through microcredit to create economic and social development from below."[8] By the end of 2011, Grameen had more than $12 billion in revenues and twenty-two thousand employees.[9] Microfinance at the bottom of the pyramid has enabled large populations to break the cycle of poverty. It is also evidence that financial inclusion can provide the poorest of the poor with tools to ensure their own economic development and can promote self-reliance through access to private capital.

There is a growing movement to actively promote and expand microfinance in the belief that such access to capital enables the poor to rise out of poverty. Microfinance can effectively promote economic development, self-reliance, and employment growth by supporting the empowerment of entrepreneurs in the developing world. As wealth increases at the bottom of the pyramid, so too do the requirements for secondary and tertiary financial services and products associated with rising prosperity, such as insurance.

Microinsurance is the protection of low-income people against specific loss.[10] According to the International Labour Organization, microinsurance has reached half a billion people. Typically, the market consists of people in the developing world previously ignored by mainstream commercial insurance companies. According to the world's oldest insurance company, Lloyds, the potential market for microinsurance is between 1.5 and 3 billion policies. It is important to recognize that insurance against loss is also a function of prosperity and industrial development. Therefore, a greater number of people in the developing world seeking to insure themselves against potential loss indicates growing economic prosperity and enhanced financial inclusion.

Since the global financial crisis, loss of confidence in the banking and financial sector has demonstrated the need for financial inclusion in industrialized economies as well as in the developing world. According to the Alliance for Financial Inclusion, there are more than thirty million people in the United States who are unbanked.[11] People in Europe are at greater risk of financial marginalization than ever before due to the sovereign debt crises and bailouts across the continent. A paradigm shift is also required in the developed world to recognize that banking is a noble cause and is as critical to ensuring prosperity and poverty reduction as eradicating malaria.

Bill Gates, cofounder of Microsoft and the Gates Foundation and perhaps the world's greatest living philanthropist,[12] agrees that financial inclusion is essential. "Innovations like vaccines and high-yielding crops have changed the future for billions of people," he said in a July 2014 article in *Forbes*.[13] According to Gates, however, "We're at the cusp of another breakthrough innovation: including the poorest in the financial system that increases, instead of limiting, the value of their assets. Transforming the underlying economics of financial services through digital currency will help those who live in poverty directly. It will also support a host of other development activities, including health and agriculture. The vision... is a paradigm shift in the way the poor are able to approach life, seizing control of it rather than trying to manage it."[14]

Gates has invested more than $28 billion in philanthropic capital to reduce poverty and eradicate malaria, in addition to actively funding financial inclusion initiatives that recognize the importance of access to financial services.[15] Access to such services plays a critical role in international development by promoting economic growth. Reducing barriers to entrepreneurship and generating prosperity at the bottom of the financial pyramid reduces income inequality and promotes self-reliance. Inclusive financial services create the vital conditions for stability in developing markets, reducing economic vulnerability and promoting employment.

Financial inclusion is about empowering the 2.5 billion people who are currently outside the formal financial services system to enter the fold.[16] The more consumers participate, the better the system performs for everyone. This mass migration of billions of new customers demanding basic access to financial services, bank accounts, deposits, insurance, and credit can be a reality within a decade. Provision of financial services ought to be considered a human right, with the entire financial services industry playing a key role in improving the state of the world. This is also a substantial new business growth opportunity for established firms in the developed world to grow market share and enhance their global footprint. Integrating the latest technology into the financial services realm will ease the expansion across the developing world, granting all consumers equal access to the latest information and inclusive finance capabilities. That is finance at its very best, empowering people to be their best selves and realize their boundless hopes and dreams. Finance is a force for good in the world, and the impact of investing is amplified significantly when the greatest numbers of people are served by broad-based financial inclusion.

## Investing in Infrastructure

Investing in infrastructure creates clear social and economic value for people everywhere, because increased public infrastructure investment can have powerful effects on the broader economy. Infrastructure investments create jobs directly and indirectly across the economy. In 2009, the Political Economy Research Institute at the University of Massachusetts Amherst estimated that for every $1 billion invested in new infrastructure, eighteen thousand jobs were created.[17] Moreover, increasing investment in infrastructure by 1 percent raises the level of total economic output by 0.4 percent of gross domestic product in the same year and 1.5 percent in the subsequent four years, according to data from the International Monetary Fund.[18] In fact, infrastructure quality is the hallmark of a well-functioning and modern economy.

Frankly, infrastructure is an asset class that has not received the recognition that it deserves in terms of generating positive social impact and financial return. In fact, infrastructure is the most attractive asset class for making large-scale impact investments because it has the capacity to attract trillions of dollars in investment capital. There is a clear public need for things like roads, hospitals, airports, railways, electrical grids, and ports. The United States has demonstrated a greater willingness to embrace private-market participation, even though historically these infrastructure assets have been built, financed, and owned by government in many developed and developing economies. However, government's core strength has invariably been in areas like service delivery, whereas its weakness has been in areas like building, financing, and owning infrastructure assets. Therefore, infrastructure investment is perhaps the optimal intersection between private capital and public need. Such public–private partnerships are a unique way for finite public resources to be deployed in a fashion that optimizes private capital and expertise. The private sector is incentivized to build the highest-quality infrastructure assets at the lowest cost in the shortest timeframe. Such incentives do not often apply to the public sector, and therefore substandard and inefficiently managed assets have been built. The importance of infrastructure as a core component and key driver of economic growth, competitiveness, and social good is well documented by institutions like the International Monetary Fund.[19]

Investments in infrastructure have substantial economic and social benefits, both in terms of the short run and the long run. There is a large body of economic research that demonstrates investments in infrastructure can have a significant positive impact on the long-run performance of an economy. For instance, research by the World Economic Forum[20] makes the case that investments that generate, maintain, or expand infrastructure networks are likely to promote increased efficiency, higher productivity, and more rapid economic growth. Despite the enormous potential for substantial long-term economic benefits from infrastructure investment, the United States has been underinvesting for many decades. The U.S. invests approximately 2 percent of GDP in infrastructure, compared with China's investment of 9 percent and Europe's of 5 percent of GDP.[21]

Governments all over the world face an acute need to upgrade, modernize, and build new infrastructure. The World Economic Forum estimates there to be an annual debt and equity investment deficit in global infrastructure of at least $1 trillion per annum.[22] This is a remarkable occurrence because there is an abundance of private-sector capital, while at the same time there are perpetual public-sector needs for infrastructure investment. Investment scarcity is not the constraint; government's will to cede control tends to be the obstacle. Since the global financial crisis, governments around the world have taken on enormous debts and significant deficits, and in some cases have bordered on insolvency. Indeed, many countries have defaulted on their debts, requiring the government to seek a bailout.

However, there is a chasm between an intention to make infrastructure investments and actual committed capital. The combined assets under management of pension funds, insurance companies, endowments, and sovereign wealth funds total approximately $50 trillion, according to the World Economic Forum. However, it has been found that 60 percent of infrastructure investors are below their target allocations, according to a survey by Prequin.[23] Astonishingly, the Organisation for Economic Co-operation and Development conducted a pension fund survey in October 2013 that found infrastructure investment classed unlisted equity at just 0.8 percent of assets under management. In a world of government financial constraint and below-trend economic growth, with private capital facing no fundamental problems of scarcity, there is clearly a massive opportunity to correct this imbalance and increase infrastructure investment.

Infrastructure investment is one of the few asset classes in which large institutional investors can deploy vast sums, in the billions, of debt and equity capital. Infrastructure is one of the best asset classes for delivering real impact that can add enormous value to society. In fact, major infrastructure investments, either greenfield or brownfield (meaning that parent companies construct new facilities in a foreign country or that companies lease existing facilities for new operations), have the capacity to add substantially greater positive social impact to society than the cumulative sum of philanthropic money, government aid, and social impact bonds. It should be noted that, however well intentioned these virtuous programs are, they tend to be narrowly focused and rarely

The government promises to pay the external organization a prearranged and agreed-upon sum of money if, and only if, the organization is able to accomplish the desired social outcome.

It is important to note that a social impact bond is not a "bond" in the traditional sense; it is not like a corporate or municipal bond, which has a fixed rate and term. In simple terms, the private-sector capital at risk is similar to a regular corporate bond; if the program is successful, the payments from government are akin to interest coupon payments. Typically, a social impact bond will also involve an additional tranche of complexity as the external organization, such as a foundation, will usually seek outside investors to participate in the investment syndicate. In this complex structure, social impact bonds are often referred to as pay-for-success bonds, reflecting the immense positive social impact of innovative financing solutions and the rigorous shared outcomes that are the basis of the contract.

The concept of a social impact bond originated in the United Kingdom in 2010.[33] The world's first social impact bond was structured to combat recidivism among three thousand short-term nonviolent offenders serving less than twelve months at Peterborough Prison.[34] Funding from investors worth £5 million, completely outside of government, was initially used to pay for services to help rehabilitate offenders through a program undertaken by external service providers with a proven track record of working successfully with prisoners. Evaluated over a six-year period, reductions in prisoner reoffending rates must be at least 7.5 percent, or investors receive no financial return from government. After four years, the project has reduced reoffending rates by 8.4 percent compared to those offenders not in the program.[35] A reduction of 10 percent would trigger immediate payment to investors. After four years, performance indicates that investors are on track to receive positive returns in 2016; as long as reductions in reoffenses remain above

7.5 percent, the government will make payments to investors.[36] Since the establishment of the first social impact bond, the United Kingdom has fostered an ecosystem of social financing, providing a template for other countries to emulate addressing different social challenges. In 2012, the government established Big Society Capital, the first British investment dedicated to supporting the social investment market, with £600 million in available capital.[37]

Social impact bonds have gradually become an accepted social financing mechanism in the United States as well. In 2013, the Goldman Sachs Urban Investment Group formed a partnership with the United Way of Salt Lake and J.B. Pritzker to create the first ever social impact bond designed to finance early childhood education.[38] J.B. Pritzker and Goldman Sachs jointly committed up to $7 million to finance the Utah High-Quality Preschool Program, essentially a targeted high-impact curriculum that focuses on increasing school readiness and academic performance among at-risk three- and four-year-olds in Utah.[39] Students who enter kindergarten better prepared are less likely to require special education and remedial services in school, saving the state of Utah money and resulting in cost savings for the school districts.[40]

Social impact bonds and other private debt instruments offer predictable financial returns and enhanced control over social benefits. These innovative financing structures also offer economies of scale, facilitating larger capital allocations. Social impact bonds can, and ought to be, structured to attract retail investor capital by offering a demonstrable positive social impact that also meets their risk and return profile. These products should be distributed through responsible sales channels, including financial advisers and brokerage firms, offering an alternative diversification source. Finance is a force for a good, and it is time to open up social impact bonds and other impact investments to everyone, including retail investors and pension funds, allowing for greater competition and far greater positive social impact.

## Philanthropy as an Asset Class

Contrary to the popular misconception that "philanthropy" means charity, the word actually derives from Latin roots meaning "love of humanity." Philanthropy has traditionally been the vehicle wealthy individuals and foundations use to dispense grant money and private capital for charitable projects. In 2013, Americans gave a total of $355.17 billion to charity. This included $241.32 billion from individuals (72 percent), $50.28 billion from foundations (15 percent), $26.81 from bequests (8 percent), and $16.76 billion from corporations (5 percent). In total, charitable giving accounted for 2 percent of U.S. GDP in 2013.[41]

Competition for a slice of the philanthropic pie is intense, and succeeding at that competition is often the difference between economic life and death for a charitable organization. For the most part, the nonprofit sector has become accustomed to annual grant applications diverting precious human resources away from the field and into the office. These onerous tasks are often time-consuming, bureaucratic, and labor-intensive, and the process tends to reward the best political operatives rather than the best practitioners. The culture in philanthropy has had a tendency to reward paternalism rather than evidence-based success. After all, for every hour spent doing paperwork there is a significant opportunity cost, as that time would otherwise be spent delivering core activities in the field.

The *2014 U.S. Trust Study of High Net Worth Philanthropy* examined the giving patterns, priorities, and attitudes of America's wealthiest households for the year 2013.[42] The product of a partnership between the U.S. Trust and the Lilly Family School of Philanthropy at Indiana University, the research study is the fifth in a series conducted over time.[43] In 2013, 98.4 percent of high-net-worth households in the United States donated to charity, compared with 95.4 percent in 2011.[44] This compares favorably to the

65 percent of the general American population who donate to charity.[45] Since the global financial crisis, private capital has become more highly sought after, and the donor market is highly competitive. As a result, sophisticated donors are also becoming more insistent on greater transparency and accountability before pledging.

According to the study, in 2013 a variety of motivations drove high-net-worth philanthropy: 73 percent believed that their gift could make a difference and 74 percent felt a sense of personal satisfaction.[46] In addition, 63 percent cited giving back to the community as a motivation, while only 34 percent of donors cited tax advantages as their motivation for giving.[47] Philanthropy has become more personalized and strategic, with 73 percent of high-net-worth American donors having a specific strategy in place to guide their charitable giving.[48] The study also found that 51 percent of households with a net worth between $1 million and $5 million, and 69 percent of households with a net worth greater than $5 million, use a giving vehicle such as a private foundation, charitable trust, or donor-advised fund to disperse their funds.[49]

Numerous single-issue philanthropic foundations are differentiated by the name of the donor rather than the cause. Resources in the sector are so scarce that duplication and inefficiency is only perpetuated by ego philanthropy rather than efficacy. According to the National Center for Charitable Statistics, there are currently more than 1.5 million nonprofit organizations in the U.S.[50] The culture is changing, however, as more entrepreneurs and successful industrialists are entering the philanthropic arena and applying corporate methodology and data metrics to nonprofit challenges.

The infusion of a more diverse pool of human capital, particularly from the for-profit business world, has greatly benefited the charitable sector and had a positive impact on reforming the culture in philanthropy. This is further evidenced by the fact that 93 percent of donors apply a certain level of focus to their charitable activity, according to the U.S. Trust study. Ultimately, the sustainability of any sector is predicated on financial resources being sufficient to meet the needs of operational expenses over time. This challenge is not unique to the philanthropic community, though there is a range of intricacies that separates the sector. By definition, the not-for-profit sector relies on profits from other areas of the economy to fund its activities. Charities, for the most part, are not run like businesses. In fact, charities are disincentivized to be run profitably because they rely on grants and donations to survive. Therefore, if they have excess grant money at year's end, a donor may feel the charity does not need the money and look elsewhere. This perception has a detrimental impact on the culture of the philanthropic sector, which ought to be as professional as any other fiduciary sector in the economy.

In the marketplace there is fierce competition for donor funds, because 84 percent of wealthy donors are aware of alternative ways to use their financial resources to advance social or charitable goals.[51] These include areas such as impact investing, social impact bonds, and specific mission-related investing. Despite this high level of awareness, only 13 percent currently use such approaches, though the trend is growing. Therefore, we are long overdue in thinking of philanthropy as an asset class. In this new framework, capital allocators will no longer think about making a one-off donation for which the probability of return is zero. In fact, capital allocators will start to think like portfolio managers making investments, where there is an expectation of a return.

Philanthropic returns come in a variety of forms, including happiness, utility, pride, achievement, and financial rewards. The U.S. Trust study found that 92 percent of respondents expressed the highest confidence in nonprofit organizations resolving domestic and global issues. This remarkable finding demonstrates a loss of faith in traditional institutions' ability to tackle such challenges. Specifically, the study found that only 54 percent had faith in the federal government and just 25 percent in Congress, indicating a bias toward the private sector as the preferred vehicle for delivering positive social impact. In fact, the study indicated that 58 percent of respondents believed that corporations were equipped to resolve global issues, while 73 percent believed that religious institutions were best suited.[52]

Such a mind-set makes every scarce philanthropic dollar accountable for a demonstrable or measurable return. This benefits the charity by enforcing evidence-based accountability, performance metrics, and transparency, and benefits the donor by encouraging a more rigorous investment approach. This would also compel philanthropic donors to apply their immense business smarts to innovative social challenges and encourage their advisors to utilize objectivity in terms of performance measurement. Therefore, thinking about philanthropy as an asset class becomes all the more important as charitable giving increases in size, scale, and sophistication in the effort to deliver positive social impact. Philanthropic capital that is allocated with an investment mind-set ensures the efficacy and long-term sustainability of giving to solve societal challenges, demonstrating the power of finance to improve the state of the world.

## Stock Market and Public Equity Investing

Impact investing has the potential to transform the lives of billions of people, deliver generous financial returns, and fundamentally transform investment markets. In order to reach its optimal potential, impact investing needs to penetrate global stock market investing. This is fundamentally important for a number of reasons, including but not limited to the fact that in 2013, 52 percent of the world's $31.98 trillion dollars in pension assets were allocated to stocks and public equity.[53] The stock market is often the only asset class many investors explore, outside of their home equity or bonds.

Public equity markets are the largest, most liquid, and best understood investment markets in the world. They are also the most visible, transparent, and accessible source of capital for many investors and corporations alike. Impact investing and the stock market have traditionally been limited to socially responsible and ethical investment approaches, negatively screening and excluding companies based on arbitrary measures. This may include an investor choosing to exclude firms that are engaged in arms manufacturing, tobacco sales, or nuclear production. These investment approaches neither incentivize nor reward companies that are intentionally generating positive social impact. In fact, they are mildly redundant, as they do not actually have any positive impact at all. Negative screening merely results in the investment boycott of certain firms and doesn't effectively change behavior. Therefore, an investment approach that encourages, incentivizes, and rewards publicly traded corporations to generate positive social impact and financial returns is paramount.

The 6E Paradigm provides an evaluative framework for any impact investor seeking to invest in the stock market. A dynamic hexagonal framework, the 6E Paradigm is a tool that impact investors can apply to their public equity investments. This is important because managers of the largest pool of investor capital—pension funds—can implement this approach for listed stock market investments. Pension funds represent the retirement savings of millions of people and are often constrained with regard to the asset classes they can invest in. Therefore, building a robust investment framework like the 6E Paradigm empowers pension funds, retail investors, sovereign wealth funds, mutual funds, and exchange-traded funds to actively and intentionally make impact investments. This approach rewards companies that are doing well by their stakeholders, society, and shareholders, and generates incentives for competitors to follow suit. It also unlocks the trillions of dollars in equity capital that has previously been outside the impact investing remit, often limited to sophisticated private debt instruments like social impact bonds that are typically available only to wealthy philanthropists. Stock markets are the optimal platform for holding company executives accountable given the public nature of the markets, and they are the most transparent as well.

Stock markets in the United States, including the S&P, Dow Jones Industrials, and NASDAQ, are the largest in the world. By virtue of the deep liquidity, transparency, and market coverage by investors, there are significant opportunities for financial innovation and product creation. This is important if impact investing is to reach its potential, as there are currently limited supplies of robust impact investment products. Further, the impact investment products available tend to be accessible only to philanthropic investors and are limited in nature. Social impact bonds, for instance, are debt-like instruments with little or no liquidity and are small in size. These investments are often available only in private markets exclusive to family office, ultra-high-net-worth, and philanthropic investors.

Opening up the potential for impact investment products based on the stock market represents a game changer for the impact investing community. The stock market vastly increases the potential market size of impact investing, but it also expands the investor base tremendously to include investors previously constrained by limited product choice or asset allocation. This market expansion encompasses pension funds investors, retail investors, and mutual funds, representing the majority of investment capital in the marketplace. It enables all investors to consider impact, consciously, purposefully, and intentionally, in their stock market investment decisions. This, in turn, effectively realigns corporate and executive incentives to actively meet impact measurements in concert with delivering shareholder returns.

The 6E Paradigm unlocks the stock market to tangible impact investment. In this brave new world, all investors who implement the 6E Paradigm are, by definition, positively influencing the allocation of capital. Investing with impact becomes second nature to investors of all sizes and risk profiles and in all geographic areas. Choosing investments using this revolutionary framework sends an important signal that good behavior and positive social impact on the part of corporations will be rewarded by investors. This new price signal therefore penalizes those corporations that take a status quo approach by failing to account for positive social impact in their activities. It is a bold step toward encouraging the culture in financial services to value holistic financial and social impact. Impact investments will grow in size from millions to billions, and the total market opportunity will expand over time from billions to trillions of dollars. The rule, rather than the exception, will be that corporations actively deliver positive social impact in conjunction with financial returns. The 6E Paradigm is real, robust, and ready for investors of all sizes and risk profiles to embrace, thus improving the state of the world by maximizing positive social impact and delivering financial returns.

## Investor Activism

As they say, "money talks." Investors are to the finance industry what voters are to politicians. Specifically, they hold all the power. By positively influencing the allocation of capital, investors have the capacity to realize the greatest impact that free markets can generate. Impact investing needs to be driven from the bottom up to have the broadest influence. The most common type of investor activism involves an individual or group purchasing a large quantity of a public company stock and then pressuring the board or management to effect major change. In most cases, a company becomes a target for activist investors if it is perceived to be mismanaged, has excessive costs, or is less profitable than investors deem reasonable. The primary aim of investor activism is to realize or unlock additional value for shareholders. In addition, activist investors have a major role to play in terms of impact investing, and they can leverage their influence to ensure that strong financial returns also correlate to positive social impact.

An activist approach to public equity investing can often produce returns in excess of those likely to be achieved with a passive investment strategy. Significantly, the top-performing activist hedge funds produced an average return some 53 percentage points greater than the MSCI World Index in the period between 2006 and 2011. According to research firm Activist Insight, the average annual net return of the leading forty activist hedge funds consistently outperformed the MSCI World Index in the years following the global financial crisis, demonstrating the power of activist investing to effect change.[54] Realizing additional value is important to the efficiency of the investment industry; unlocking marginal profit also unearths new opportunities to open up areas that will lead to greater positive social impact.

Given the sheer size, status, and immense power of corporations in society, businesses have a unique obligation to act in the best interests of humanity and be a source of good, even if there is a potentially adverse effect on profitability. In other words, businesses have a voluntary responsibility to act in accordance with societal values. One of the most intriguing attributes of the free market is the interaction between corporations and their most powerful stakeholders: their shareholders. Shareholders, collectively, are considered the owners of a corporation, and have become some of the most powerful allies and important advocates for enhanced corporate social responsibility. Shareholder and investor activism is a reflection of changing societal attitudes and has played a key role in civil rights and environmental debates over the years. Activist shareholder groups are moving beyond pure investment by proposing specific resolutions at the annual general meeting and mobilizing other shareholders to support, or oppose, key resolutions. These groups use shareholder resolutions as well as other means of pressure to address issues that may not necessarily be first-order business priorities. This form of investor activism is forging a new model of responsible ownership whereby good corporate citizenship is premised upon a democratic shareholder decision-making process.

Increased shareholder lobbying activity challenges the key assumption that extracting maximum value and shareholder returns are the most important considerations. Therein lies the challenge for corporate executives, who must balance social and economic pressures. This challenge becomes much more difficult when the economic and social interests of an activist investor are aligned, and the lines between social activist and financial investor are blurred. Increasingly, shareholder activism is shifting from a vocal minority of private investors to the large institutional investors, including pension and sovereign wealth funds heavily influenced by nongovernmental organizations with political or economic links. Board members of such large institutional investors are ultimately responsible for the investment decisions of the underlying funds and are increasingly risk averse and concerned about reputational risk and their fiduciary responsibility.

There is an inflection point at which corporate executives begin to act more like politicians and less like corporate executives if investor activism becomes overtly political. This critical point has long passed, and too many corporate executives are more concerned with the equivalent of corporate opinion polls and media popularity than with shareholder returns. Corporate executives are ultimately judged on their results, measured in financial and shareholder returns. Executives must, therefore, proactively realize the financial benefits of good corporate citizenship and of delivering positive social impact. Starbucks Corporation is one organization that has deftly balanced the desire to deliver enormous positive social impact for employees, farmers, customers, and the community, while delivering substantial shareholder value along the way.

Investor and shareholder activism has been far more successful at delivering increased financial returns than it has been at solving grand social challenges. Until now, much of the shareholder activism has centered on the corporate environmental footprint, and these efforts have had limited success. This is unfortunate, as the world has debated environmental issues for multiple decades at the multilateral political level with virtually no material success.

Corporations have a unique role to play in creating a cleaner environment, and they also have economic incentives to use energy more efficiently as demand and costs rise globally. If every company in the S&P 500 voluntarily reported and disclosed its energy costs, clearly and explicitly as a line item on the balance sheet, there would be pressure to reduce that cost, just as there is for every other expense item. This would result in analyst and investor pressure on corporate executives to be more efficient with their energy output and to source cheaper and alternative sources, which would have a far greater impact on carbon emissions and pollution than any political treaty in history. As an added advantage, reducing costs increases profitability, which provides the appropriate incentives for corporate executives to act in their shareholders' best interests and effect positive social change. According to PwC, 98 percent of the S&P 500 companies surveyed can link investments in emissions reduction to value creation.[55] As a result, these corporations are discovering new ways to enhance efficiencies, create new markets, and build a competitive advantage.

In the world before the global financial crisis, externalities were often mispriced or not priced at all, and corporations were able to shift these costs to government and consumers. However, the world has changed due to public-sector capital constraints and to other social issues that need to be addressed. Now there is greater emphasis on the private sector to share the burden and effect change. Investor activism is a core part of the impact investing landscape and a worthy investment approach that unlocks enhanced shareholder value while delivering demonstrable positive social impact.

## Enlightened Self-Interest and Free Markets

Free markets have delivered prosperity to billions of people. In order for finance to fulfill its potential and deliver the tools to continue this prosperous evolution, financial inclusion needs to reach the billions of people at the bottom of the economic pyramid who are currently underserved by the financial system. The free market system is broad based, with ample capacity to integrate and foster the best of human endeavor by actively encouraging the 2.5 billion people currently outside the formal financial services system to join the community of citizens who are participating and flourishing. When financial inclusion reaches its zenith, hopefully in the next decade, the world will be a more stable, secure, and prosperous place for all people. At that point, free markets can work best by facilitating the talents and entrepreneurship of people everywhere, and finance can then play its part as a force for good on an even grander scale.

Financial inclusion means the global pie gets bigger, and when the world financial system fully integrates the bottom and top of the economic pyramid, the capacity for massive infrastructure investment is all the more attractive to the vast pools of private-sector capital. Governments will be empowered to partner with the private sector to divest non-core infrastructure assets and build new and improved infrastructure that will last for the next hundred years as populations continue to evolve and become prosperous. Building vital new infrastructure in the developing world will raise living standards, increase productivity, reduce corruption, and generate sustainable intergenerational prosperity. Infrastructure investment sends the appropriate price signal to major investors by providing the right incentives to invest, to transform, and to have the greatest positive social impact.

Investing in infrastructure is big and bold. It can easily put trillions of dollars to work, and can have long-term positive social impact at the macro scale. On the micro level, the private-sector organizations can have enormous positive impact by partnering with government and philanthropists, structuring pay-for-success financial instruments like social impact bonds. These sophisticated investments are new and relatively small today, but with time and greater success, they can easily be scaled to attract significantly greater pools of investment capital. Paying for success is a revolutionary business model for the public sector, and can pave the way for public–private partnership funding for the next century.

Ultimately, the full impact of investment will be driven from the bottom up. Positively influencing the allocation of capital means investors must take responsibility and actively participate in the process. Information asymmetry—the availability of information to one party in a transaction that is not available to the other—is no longer a constraint to an activist investment philosophy. Investor activism delivers enhanced financial returns but also generates greater positive social impact. Generating higher returns for investors is important, as it underwrites the ability to pursue nonprofit passions. Private-sector corporations are equipped to deal with public policy challenges with greater efficacy and more measurable success than the public sector, for the most part. Private-sector organizations have an important role to play as good corporate citizens that deliver superior financial returns to shareholders and responsibly allocate resources to deliver optimal positive social impact.

The impact of investing is optimal for investors and society when we positively influence the allocation of capital. There is a financial premium for doing good. This is finance at its most innovative, at its most impactful, at its best. Finance is fundamentally a force for good in the world. In fact, free markets empowered by people pursuing the ethical path of enlightened self-interest have delivered the greatest positive social impact the world has ever seen.

# Conclusion

# We, the People

Freedom is that which is morally right, and it forms the foundation that underwrites our most basic human rights. It is time for people to regain control of their economic destiny. Capitalism is a metaphor for freedom and is the greatest force for prosperity and opportunity the world has ever known. It has raised more than a billion people from extreme poverty to the path of prosperity in the last quarter-century alone. Today, there are more than 4.5 billion people on the planet who believe in the superiority of the free market capitalist system.[1] Enlightened self-interest empowers people to choose the path that benefits both themselves and others, while free markets are typically found together with freedom of speech, religion, movement, association, and ideas.

Modern history has demonstrated that if those who pull the levers of our financial systems display poor ethical and moral judgment, they can do immense economic and social damage. Income inequality has decreased across countries, but increased within them. In other words, more people around the world are getting equally poorer while a minority gets vastly richer. Real wages have not moved higher in fifty years in the United States, as inequality continues to grow.[2] This process has been driven by a combination of structural factors like government economic policy failures and technology that increases productivity and replaces humans.[3]

In normal times, government fiscal policy is supported by central bank monetary policy working in tandem to offset economic imbalances. Between 2009 and 2012, the U.S. Congress and Senate had difficulty reaching a compromise and passing the annual budget, and the Federal Reserve has implemented quantitative easing monetary policies, keeping interest rates near zero. These are abnormal times, but the extraordinary economic policy measures have made problems worse. In fact, the quantitative easing policy "hasn't been a success," according to former Federal Reserve chairman Alan Greenspan.[4] The trillions of dollars in spending have delivered very little to the people on Main Street but have been enormously profitable for those who needed economic stimulus the least. The richest percentile of the world's population now owns more than 48.2 percent of global wealth, according to the *Credit Suisse Wealth Report.*[5] In fact, the richest eighty-five people across the globe are worth the equivalent combined wealth of the poorest 3.5 billion people on the planet.[6]

In the developed world, the income and opportunity inequality problems are even more pronounced, requiring comprehensive solutions driven by the private sector as the engine for economic growth. When government is weak, society needs business to be strong. The banking and finance sector has the capacity to facilitate financial capital flow, enabling businesses to invest, create jobs, deliver prosperity, and increase the overall size of the economic pie. That is the profound role of the finance sector in the capitalist system, to fundamentally deliver the resources required to improve the state of the world. Therefore, impact investing is the investment approach best placed to realize these ambitions by intentionally delivering measurable positive social impact and generating profit.

However, impact investing is much easier to talk about than it is to implement successfully. It has become the feel-good term for many well-intentioned stakeholders, including government, philanthropists, and businesses that have devoted exponentially more words to the cause than money.[7] After all, more than $13 trillion in assets are managed in investment funds that have progressive investment mandates to account for social impact, yet the total size of the impact investment market is only $40 billion.[8] Moreover, there are 1,200 asset managers, advising $45 trillion in financial capital, who are signatories to the United Nations Principles for Responsible Investment.[9] Where is the accountability for matching words with action? The impact investing market is led by a belief that social impact bonds are the optimal investment approach, but they are labor intensive to structure and small in scale, with the majority of investors unable to participate. Government inertia is another costly stumbling block. Therefore, democratizing impact investing and making it accessible, tangible, and efficient is the solution to attracting the trillions in mainstream investment capital.

In the capitalist system, the stock exchange enables investors to provide the financial capital to companies seeking to raise money. Investors become the owners of those companies by providing the liquidity the firms need to grow in a transparent marketplace. It is also the asset class most attractive to investors of all shapes and sizes. In August 2014, the combined market capitalization of world stock exchanges was more than $64 trillion,[10] with over 52 percent of the $31.98 trillion in global pension fund assets invested in the stock market.[11]

This represents the opportunity for impact investing to have the greatest possible impact by actively penetrating the global stock and equity markets. The status quo in finance will only change when there is an economic incentive to do good rather than a market that is indifferent to social impact. Good companies are those that are profitable and deliver positive social impact. Bad companies, however, focus on profits without concern for the broader impact they are having on society. The global financial crisis dealt a harsh reality check for the firms led by executives who embodied myopic selfishness and expressed supreme disrespect for other stakeholders. The world is crying out for leadership in uncertain times, and the leaders who display moral courage will be those remembered favorably by history.

## Positively Influencing the Allocation of Capital

The entire banking and finance industry has a unique opportunity to be at the forefront of perhaps the most important philosophical shift in cultural values in the history of humankind. According to United Nations estimates, the current world population of 7.125 billion people will reach 8.2 billion by 2025 and 9.6 billion by 2050.[12] The economic and social challenges of today will be meek compared to those in the next quarter-century.

Government has proven manifestly incapable of generating sustainable wealth and prosperity; therefore, only the private sector can achieve this. The finance industry has a core role to play in this regard, by allocating capital and providing investment resources to empower enlightened corporations to continue creating employment, embracing innovation, generating wealth, and having positive social impact. Impact investing is the avenue to explore—not as a fringe investment approach, but rather as a core value. Society will be the greatest beneficiary if, and I hope when, the finance industry embraces these trends and develops innovative concepts to positively influence the allocation of capital. In so doing, the finance industry can serve as a great vehicle for good by meeting the growing demand for impact investing products and services. This means unlocking the stock market and other asset classes to actively measure positive social impact alongside financial returns. This creates the financial incentive for corporations to act in the best interests of society and with enlightened self-interest. Good corporate behavior should always be rewarded by investors and the market.

If current trends hold, millennials will fundamentally upend corporate America and Wall Street. By 2020, there will be 103 million millennials who will make up 36 percent of the adult population, 40 percent of eligible voters, and roughly half the workforce in the United States.[13] Millennials will therefore determine the direction of America economically, politically, and culturally.[14] There is no time like the present for the finance industry to wholeheartedly embrace the changing landscape. Over the next few decades, the largest intergenerational wealth transfer in history will take place, with an estimated $41 trillion passing from baby boomers to their children and grandchildren.[15] Millennials value improving society above delivering profits as the primary responsibility of business.[16]

Over time, millennials' access to financial capital will grow and their influence will strengthen, meaning that millennials will expect their investments to be aligned with their values. Wall Street, banks, investors, pension funds, philanthropists, and the finance industry as a whole can either lead the effort today or watch this once-in-a-generation opportunity to improve the state of the world sail by.

*We can no longer afford to wait.*

# Acknowledgments

The impetus to write this book began on October 25, 2013, after I delivered a TEDx talk titled "The Noble Cause: Positively Influencing the Allocation of Capital." It has since been viewed online over a quarter million times and feedback from around the world has been overwhelming. The outpouring of support from people across all walks of life to continue to deliver this message of hope, effectively making the case that finance can be a force for good, has repeatedly inspired me along this journey.

There are many people who made this project come to life and therefore deserve an expression of my deep gratitude.

May I begin with special mention to the entire team at my publisher, Bibliomotion, so ably led by Jill Friedlander and Erika Heilman. Thanks for your tremendous support, editing prowess, encouragement, and dedication to seeing this project come to light.

Thanks to my agent for this project, Book Marketing International, led by Linda Langton.

Adjunct Professor Donald M. Krueger, you have been a tremendous friend, mentor, and wise counsel over the course of this journey, for which I am truly grateful.

I want to pay tribute to all the brave men and women who provided source materials and insight throughout the interview, research, and writing process. My only hope is that the culture of silence ends, and you can one day feel empowered to speak freely without fear or favor.

On a very personal level I wish to acknowledge my parents, David and Rosemary Balkin. My command of the English language is insufficient to accurately articulate my feelings towards you and express gratitude for the immense love, values, and wisdom you have imparted throughout my life.

The person who has been most loyal, trustworthy, and committed throughout this entire experience has been my wife, Rebecca. Sincere thanks for the love and inspiration to see this dream partnership evolve into reality. May the light you shine continue to bless all those around you.

Finally I want to thank you, the reader. Time is the most precious non-renewable resource there is because this moment is all we have. Thanks for committing the time and energy to read this book in its entirety. I hope the ideas expressed are able to inspire you to take action and commit to improving the state of the world, because finance *is* a force for good.

# Notes

## Introduction

1. Josh Fineman and Yalman Onaran, “Lehman Brothers’ Corporate History and Chronology: Timeline,” *Bloomberg*, September 15, 2008, accessed October 1, 2014, http://www.bloomberg.com/apps/news?pid=newsarchive&sid=a63mWc3ILlTo.
2. Christopher Condon, “Reserve Primary Money Fund Falls Below $1 a Share (Update4),” *Bloomberg*, September 16, 2008, accessed October 1, 2014, http://www.bloomberg.com/apps/news?pid=newsarchive&sid=a5O2y1go1GRU.
3. Pedro Nicolacida Da Costa, “Bernanke: 2008 Meltdown Was Worse Than Great Depression,” *Wall Street Journal*, August 26, 2014, accessed October 1, 2014, http://blogs.wsj.com/economics/2014/08/26/2008-meltdown-was-worse-than-great-depression-bernanke-says/?mod=WSJ_hp_Europe_EditorsPicks.
4. Pedro Nicolacida Da Costa, “Bernanke: 2008 Meltdown Was Worse Than Great Depression,” *Wall Street Journal*, August 26, 2014, accessed October 1, 2014, http://blogs.wsj.com/economics/2014/08/26/2008-meltdown-was-worse-than-great-depression-bernanke-says/?mod=WSJ_hp_Europe_EditorsPicks.
5. Pedro Nicolacida Da Costa, “Bernanke: 2008 Meltdown Was Worse Than Great Depression,” *Wall Street Journal*, August 26, 2014, accessed October 1, 2014, http://blogs.wsj.com/economics/2014/08/26/2008-meltdown-was-worse-than-great-depression-bernanke-says/?mod=WSJ_hp_Europe_EditorsPicks.
6. James Taylor, “Climategate 2.0: New E-Mails Rock the Global Warming Debate,” *Forbes Online*, November 23, 2011, accessed October 1,

2014, http://www.forbes.com/sites/jamestaylor/2011/11/23/climategate-2-0-new-e-mails-rock-the-global-warming-debate/.

7. "CNN Library: UK Phone Hacking Scandal Fast Facts," accessed October 1, 2014, http://www.cnn.com/2013/10/24/world/europe/uk-phone-hacking-scandal-fast-facts/.
8. Andrew W. Lehren and Scott Shane, "Leaked Cables Offer Raw Look at U.S. Diplomacy," *New York Times,* November 28, 2010, accessed October 1, 2014, http://www.nytimes.com/2010/11/29/world/29cables.html?pagewanted=all&_r=0.
9. Alice Gomstyn and Brian Ross, "Lehman Brothers Boss Defends $484 Million in Salary, Bonus," *ABC News*, October 6, 2008, accessed October 1, 2014, http://abcnews.go.com/Blotter/story?id=5965360.
10. Dov Seidman, "Capitalism for Everyone or No One," *Forbes Online*, May 26, 2014, accessed October 1, 2014, http://www.forbes.com/sites/dovseidman/2014/05/26/capitalism-for-everyone-or-no-one/.
11. James Pethokoukis, "Yet Again, Obama Shows He Doesn't Quite 'Get' Why Free Enterprise Is So Important," American Enterprise Institute, accessed October 25, 2014, http://www.aei-ideas.org/2014/10/yet-again-obama-shows-he-doesnt-quite-get-why-free-enterprise-is-so-important-so-let-me-explain/.
12. Tina Aridas and Valentina Pasquali, "Unemployment Rates in Countries Around the World," *Global Finance*, March 13, 2013, accessed October 1, 2014, http://www.gfmag.com/global-data/economic-data/worlds-unemployment-ratescom#axzz2jgwOgMqA.
13. Foo Yun Chee, "EU Fines JPMorgan, UBS, Credit Suisse for Taking Part in Cartels," *Reuters*, October 21, 2014, accessed October 21, 2014, http://www.reuters.com/article/2014/10/21/us-libor-banks-fine-eu-idUSKCN0IA18120141021.
14. Ben Eisen, "Three Banks to Be Fined by EU for Libor-Rigging: Report," *MarketWatch,* October 21, 2014, accessed October 21, 2014, http://www.marketwatch.com/story/three-banks-to-be-fined-by-eu-for-libor-rigging-report-2014-10-21.
15. Gavin Finch, Elena Logutenkova, and Liam Vaughan, "Swiss Regulators Probing Alleged Currency Manipulation," *Bloomberg,* October 5, 2013, accessed October 1, 2014, http://www.bloomberg.com/news/2013-10-04/swiss-regulator-probes-alleged-foreign-exchange-manipulation.html.
16. Liam Vaughan, "Gold Fix Study Shows Signs of Decade of Bank Manipulation," *Bloomberg,* March 1, 2014, accessed October 1, 2014,

http://www.bloomberg.com/news/2014-02-28/gold-fix-study-shows-signs-of-decade-of-bank-manipulation.html.
17. Kevin Roose, "Is Goldman Sachs a 'Boys' Club'? This Lawsuit Claims It Is," *New York*, July 2, 2014, accessed October 1, 2014, http://nymag.com/daily/intelligencer/2014/07/goldman-sachs-a-boys-club.html.
18. R.P. Siegel, "What Is Wall Street's Frat Boy Culture Doing to Our Planet?," *Triple Pundit*, December 31, 2013, accessed October 1, 2014, http://www.triplepundit.com/2013/12/wall-streets-frat-boy-culture-planet/.
19. "Rasmussen Report: 53% Confident in U.S. Banking System," accessed October 21, 2014, http://www.rasmussenreports.com/public_content/business/general_business/october_2014/53_confident_in_u_s_banking_system.
20. Saabira Chaudhuri, "Banks' Legal Tab Still Running Higher," *Wall Street Journal Blogs*, July 23, 2014, accessed October 1, 2014, http://blogs.wsj.com/moneybeat/category/investment-banks/page/11/.
21. David Madland and Ruy Teixeira, *"New Progressive America: The Millennial Generation,"* Center for American Progress, May 13, 2009, accessed October 1, 2014, http://www.americanprogress.org/issues/progressive-movement/report/2009/05/13/6133/new-progressive-america-the-millennial-generation/.
22. *Towers Watson: Global Pension Assets Study 2014,* January 2014, accessed October 1, 2014, http://conferences.pionline.com/assets/2014_GPAS_Study_Final.pdf.
23. *Morgan Stanley: Investing with Impact,* accessed October 1, 2014, http://www.morganstanley.com/globalcitizen/pdf/investing-with-impact.pdf?v=07112013.
24. *World Economic Forum: From the Margins to the Mainstream,* September 2013, accessed October 1, 2014, http://www3.weforum.org/docs/WEF_II_FromMarginsMainstream_Report_2013.pdf.

## Chapter 1

1. Ben S. Bernanke, "Fostering Financial Stability" (speech at the 2012 Federal Reserve Bank of Atlanta Financial Markets Conference, Stone Mountain, Georgia, April 9, 2012), accessed October 1, 2014, http://www.federalreserve.gov/newsevents/speech/bernanke20120409a.htm.
2. "It's Unfair and Wrong to Label All Bankers 'Evil'," *Financial Times*, February 17, 2014, accessed October 1, 2014, http://www

.ft.com/intl/cms/s/0/506d414a-97ee-11e3-ab60-00144feab7de.html#axzz3FOCYNNjn.

3. "25 People to Blame for the Financial Crisis," *Time*, February 2009, accessed October 1, 2014, http://content.time.com/time/specials/packages/article/0,28804,1877351_1877350_1877339,00.html.
4. Matt Taibbi, "The Great American Bubble Machine," *Rolling Stone*, April 5, 2010, accessed October 1, 2014, http://www.rollingstone.com/politics/news/the-great-american-bubble-machine-20100405.
5. Halah Touryalai, "Goldman Sachs: No Longer Enemy #1," *Forbes Online*, August 10, 2012, accessed October 1, 2014, http://www.forbes.com/sites/halahtouryalai/2012/08/10/goldman-sachs-no-longer-enemy-number-one/.
6. "Anti-Defamation League—Anti-Semitic Incidents Decline for Fourth Straight Year in U.S., According to Annual ADL Audit," June 1, 2009, accessed October 1, 2014, http://archive.adl.org/presrele/asus_12/5537_12.html#.VDLjq_na6m4.
7. Neil Malhotra and Yotam Margalit, "State of the Nation: Anti-Semitism and the Economic Crisis," *Boston Review*, May/June 2009, accessed October 1, 2014, http://new.bostonreview.net/BR34.3/malhotra_margalit.php.
8. Ruth R. Wisse, *Jews and Power* (New York: Schocken Books, 2007), 188.
9. *"A Portrait of Jewish Americans,"* Pew Research Center, October 1, 2013, accessed October 1, 2014, http://www.pewforum.org/2013/10/01/jewish-american-beliefs-attitudes-culture-survey/.
10. *The Lost Decade of the Middle Class,* Pew Research Center, August 22, 2012, accessed October 1, 2014, http://www.pewsocialtrends.org/2012/08/22/the-lost-decade-of-the-middle-class/.
11. *Catholic Encyclopedia,* s.v. "Joseph-Marie, Comte de Maistre" (Robert Appleton Company, 1913).
12. *The Lost Decade of the Middle Class,* Pew Research Center, August 22, 2012, accessed October 1, 2014, http://www.pewsocialtrends.org/2012/08/22/the-lost-decade-of-the-middle-class/.
13. Paul Hannon, "After Rule Changes, Focus Shifts to Ethics of Banking," *Wall Street Journal*, October 12, 2014, accessed October 12, 2014, http://blogs.wsj.com/economics/2014/10/12/after-rule-changes-focus-shifts-to-ethics-of-banking/.
14. Paul Hannon, "After Rule Changes, Focus Shifts to Ethics of Banking," *Wall Street Journal*, October 12, 2014, accessed October 12, 2014,

http://blogs.wsj.com/economics/2014/10/12/after-rule-changes-focus-shifts-to-ethics-of-banking/.

15. Constitution of the United States, article I, section 1, accessed October 1, 2014, http://www.senate.gov/civics/constitution_item/constitution.htm.
16. "Michael Bloomberg: 'It Was Not the Banks that Created the Mortgage Crisis,'" *Huffington Post,* November 1, 2011, accessed October 1, 2014, http://www.huffingtonpost.com/2011/11/01/occupy-wall-street-michael-bloomberg-congress_n_1070342.html.
17. Jordan Weissmann, "How Wall Street Devoured Corporate America," *Atlantic,* March 5, 2013, accessed October 1, 2014, http://www.theatlantic.com/business/archive/2013/03/how-wall-street-devoured-corporate-america/273732/.
18. Benjamin Landy, "Graph: How the Financial Sector Consumed America's Economic Growth," *Century Foundation,* February 25, 2013, accessed October 1, 2014, http://tcf.org/blog/detail/graph-how-the-financial-sector-consumed-americas-economic-growth.
19. Robin Greenwood and David Scharfstein, *Harvard Business School and NBER: The Growth of Modern Finance,* July 2012, accessed October 1, 2014, http://www.people.hbs.edu/dscharfstein/growth_of_modern_finance.pdf.
20. Barry Ritholtz, *Bailout Nation: How Greed and Easy Money Corrupted Wall Street and Shook the World Economy* (New York: Wiley, 2009).
21. Michael Corkery and Fawn Johnson, "Former Bear Stearns CEO: Leverage Was Too High," *Wall Street Journal,* May 6, 2010, accessed October 1, 2014, http://online.wsj.com/news/articles/SB10001424052748703961104575226121352534794.
22. Ing-Haw Cheng, Harrison Hong, and Jose A. Scheinkman, *Yesterday's Heroes: Compensation and Creative Risk-Taking,* National Bureau of Economic Research Working Paper 16176, July 2010, accessed October 1, 2014, http://www.nber.org/papers/w16176.
23. Scott Lanman and Michael McKee, "Greenspan Says U.S. Should Consider Breaking Up Large Banks," *Bloomberg,* October 15, 2009, accessed October 1, 2014, http://www.bloomberg.com/apps/news?pid=newsarchive&sid=aJ8HPmNUfchg.
24. Abraham Lincoln, "The Gettysburg Address" (speech given November 19, 1863, at the dedication of the cemetery at Gettysburg), accessed

October 1, 2014, http://www.d.umn.edu/~rmaclin/gettysburg-address.html.

25. Henry Blodget, "No Conflict, No Interest: John Doerr, Twitter, and the Rise of Secondary Private Markets," *Business Insider,* March 11, 2011, accessed October 1, 2014, http://www.businessinsider.com/no-conflict-no-interest-john-doerr-twitter-2011-3#ixzz3KmXkUHTK.
26. James Salmon, "Greedy Bankers STILL Don't Get It," *Daily Mail* (U.K.), November 29, 2013, accessed October 1, 2014, http://www.dailymail.co.uk/news/article-2515787/Greedy-bankers-STILL-dont-Bonus-culture-returns-vengeance-years-crash-2-700-British-bankers-pocket-average-1-6million.html.
27. Saabira Chaudhuri, "Banks' Legal Tab Still Running Higher," *Wall Street Journal,* online edition, July 23, 2014, accessed October 1, 2014, http://blogs.wsj.com/moneybeat/category/investment-banks/page/11/.
28. Paul Hannon, "After Rule Changes, Focus Shifts to Ethics of Banking," *Wall Street Journal,* online edition, October 12, 2014, accessed October 12, 2014, http://blogs.wsj.com/economics/2014/10/12/after-rule-changes-focus-shifts-to-ethics-of-banking/.
29. Paul Hannon, "After Rule Changes, Focus Shifts to Ethics of Banking," *Wall Street Journal,* online edition, October 12, 2014, accessed October 12, 2014, http://blogs.wsj.com/economics/2014/10/12/after-rule-changes-focus-shifts-to-ethics-of-banking/.
30. Saabira Chaudhuri, "Banks' Legal Tab Still Running Higher," *Wall Street Journal*, July 23, 2014, accessed October 1, 2014, http://blogs.wsj.com/moneybeat/category/investment-banks/page/11/.
31. Steph Cockroft, "Pope Francis Claims Global Economy Is Close to Collapse and Describes Youth Unemployment Rates as an 'Atrocity' in Damning Message," *Daily Mail* (U.K.), June 14, 2014, accessed October 1, 2014, http://www.dailymail.co.uk/news/article-2657724/Pope-Francis-claims-global-economy-close-collapse-describes-youth-unemployment-rates-atrocity-damning-message.html.
32. "What We Believe," Inclusive Capitalism Initiative, accessed October 9, 2014, http://www.inclusivecapitalism.org/what-we-believe/.
33. "Conscious Capitalism Home Page," Conscious Capitalism, accessed October 9, 2014, http://www.consciouscapitalism.org/.
34. Nicholas Kristof, "A Nation of Takers?," *New York Times,* March 27, 2014, accessed October 1, 2014, http://www.nytimes.com/2014/03/27/opinion/kristof-a-nation-of-takers.html?_r=0.

35. M. Todd Henderson and Anup Malani, "Capitalism 2.0," *Forbes*, February 22, 2008, accessed October 1, 2014, http://www.forbes.com/forbes/2008/0310/030.html.
36. "Emerging and Developing Economies Much More Optimistic than Rich Countries about the Future," Pew Research Center, accessed October 9, 2014, http://www.pewglobal.org/2014/10/09/emerging-and-developing-economies-much-more-optimistic-than-rich-countries-about-the-future/.

## Chapter 2

1. "GDP," World Bank, accessed October 1, 2014, http://data.worldbank.org/indicator/NY.GDP.MKTP.CD.
2. "World Economic and Financial Surveys," International Monetary Fund, accessed October 1, 2014, http://www.imf.org/external/pubs/ft/weo/2009/02/weodata/index.aspx.
3. Larry Elliott, "IMF Says Economic Growth May Never Return to Pre-Crisis Levels," *Guardian* (Manchester), October 7, 2014, http://www.theguardian.com/business/2014/oct/07/imf-economic-growth-forecasts-downgraded-crisis.
4. Garrett Hardin, "The Tragedy of the Commons," *Science*, vol. 162, no. 3859, 1243–1248, December 13, 1968, accessed October 1, 2014, http://www.sciencemag.org/content/162/3859/1243.full.
5. "Quotes from Abraham Lincoln," Lincoln Archives, Inc., accessed October 1, 2014, http://lincolnarchives.com/LincolnQuotes.php.
6. David Madland and Ruy Teixeira, "New Progressive America: The Millennial Generation," Center for American Progress, May 13, 2009, accessed October 1, 2014, http://www.americanprogress.org/issues/progressive-movement/report/2009/05/13/6133/new-progressive-america-the-millennial-generation/.
7. "So How Many Millennials Are There in the U.S., Anyway?," MarketingCharts, June 30, 2014, accessed October 1, 2014, http://www.marketingcharts.com/wp/traditional/so-how-many-millennials-are-there-in-the-us-anyway-30401/.
8. "The Financial Crisis That Could Bankrupt America and the Millennial Generation," Yahoo Finance, October 16, 2013, accessed October 1, 2014, http://finance.yahoo.com/blogs/daily-ticker/financial-crisis-could-bankrupt-america-millennial-generation-163123756.html.

9. Scott Burns and Laurence J. Kotlikoff, *The Coming Generational Storm: What You Need to Know about America's Economic Future* (Cambridge, MA: The MIT Press, 2005).
10. *Millennials in Adulthood*, Pew Research Center, accessed October 1, 2014, http://www.pewsocialtrends.org/2014/03/07/millennials-in-adulthood/.
11. *Millennials in Adulthood,* Pew Research Center, accessed October 1, 2014, http://www.pewsocialtrends.org/2014/03/07/millennials-in-adulthood/.
12. Michael Hais and Morley Winograd, *How Millennials Could Upend Wall Street and Corporate America,* Brookings, May 2014, accessed October 1, 2014, http://www.brookings.edu/~/media/research/files/papers/2014/05/millennials%20wall%20st/brookings_winogradv5.pdf.
13. David Madland and Ruy Teixeira, *New Progressive America: The Millennial Generation,* Center for American Progress, May 13, 2009, accessed October 1, 2014, http://www.americanprogress.org/issues/progressive-movement/report/2009/05/13/6133/new-progressive-america-the-millennial-generation/.
14. Jeanne Meister, "Three Reasons You Need to Adopt a Millennial Mindset Regardless of Your Age," *Forbes Online,* October 5, 2012, accessed October 1, 2014, http://www.forbes.com/sites/jeannemeister/2012/10/05/millennialmindse/.
15. Annie Lowrey, "Do Millennials Stand a Chance in the Real World?," *New York Times,* March 26, 2013, accessed October 1, 2014, http://www.nytimes.com/2013/03/31/magazine/do-millennials-stand-a-chance-in-the-real-world.html?pagewanted=all&_r=0.
16. Annie Lowrey, "Do Millennials Stand a Chance in the Real World?," *New York Times,* March 26, 2013, accessed October 1, 2014, http://www.nytimes.com/2013/03/31/magazine/do-millennials-stand-a-chance-in-the-real-world.html?pagewanted=all&_r=0.
17. Paul Taylor, *The Next America: Boomers, Millennials, and the Looming Generational Showdown* (New York: PublicAffairs, 2014).
18. Paul Taylor, *The Next America: Boomers, Millennials, and the Looming Generational Showdown* (New York: PublicAffairs, 2014).
19. *Millennials in Adulthood,* Pew Research Center: accessed October 1, 2014, http://www.pewsocialtrends.org/2014/03/07/millennials-in-adulthood/.
20. *Millennials in Adulthood,* Pew Research Center, accessed October 1, 2014, http://www.pewsocialtrends.org/2014/03/07/millennials-in-adulthood/.
21. Derek Thompson, "Study: Millennials Deeply Confused About Their Politics, Finances, and Culture," *Atlantic*, March 7, 2014, accessed

October 1, 2014, http://www.theatlantic.com/business/archive/2014/03/study-millennials-deeply-confused-about-their-politics-finances-and-culture/284277/.

22. "Economic News Release," Bureau of Labor Statistics, accessed October 1, 2014, http://www.bls.gov/news.release/empsit.nr0.htm.
23. Ray Williams, "Is Gen Y Becoming the New 'Lost Generation'?," LinkedIn, July 13, 2014, accessed October 1, 2014, https://www.linkedin.com/today/post/article/20140713132101-1011572-is-gen-y-becoming-the-new-lost-generation?trk=tod-home-art-list-large_0.
24. *Millennials in Adulthood,* Pew Research Center, accessed October 1, 2014, http://www.pewsocialtrends.org/2014/03/07/millennials-in-adulthood/.
25. Aaron Kaufman, "The Second Lost Generation: Why So Many Millennials Are Failing to Launch," *Elite Daily*, February 11, 2014, accessed October 1, 2014, http://elitedaily.com/life/the-second-lost-generation-why-so-many-millennials-are-failing-to-launch/.
26. Aaron Kaufman, "The Second Lost Generation: Why So Many Millennials Are Failing to Launch," *Elite Daily*, February 11, 2014, accessed October 1, 2014, http://elitedaily.com/life/the-second-lost-generation-why-so-many-millennials-are-failing-to-launch/.
27. Ray Williams, "Is Gen Y Becoming the New 'Lost Generation'?," LinkedIn, July 13, 2014, accessed October 1, 2014, https://www.linkedin.com/today/post/article/20140713132101-1011572-is-gen-y-becoming-the-new-lost-generation?trk=tod-home-art-list-large_0.
28. *The Youth Employment Crisis: A Call for Action*, International Labour Office (Resolution and conclusions of the 101st session of the International Labour Conference), Geneva 2012, accessed October 1, 2014, http://www.ilo.org/wcmsp5/groups/public/---ed_norm/---relconf/documents/meetingdocument/wcms_185950.pdf.
29. "Poverty Overview," World Bank, accessed October 1, 2014, http://www.worldbank.org/en/topic/poverty/overview.
30. *The Youth Employment Crisis: A Call for Action*, International Labour Office (Resolution and conclusions of the 101st session of the International Labour Conference), Geneva 2012, accessed October 1, 2014, http://www.ilo.org/wcmsp5/groups/public/---ed_norm/---relconf/documents/meetingdocument/wcms_185950.pdf.
31. *The Youth Employment Crisis: A Call for Action*, International Labour Office (Resolution and conclusions of the 101st session of the International Labour Conference), Geneva 2012, accessed October 1, 2014,

http://www.ilo.org/wcmsp5/groups/public/---ed_norm/---relconf/documents/meetingdocument/wcms_185950.pdf.

32. Steph Cockroft, "Pope Francis Claims Global Economy Is Close to Collapse and Describes Youth Unemployment Rates As an 'Atrocity' in Damning Message," *Daily Mail,* June 14, 2014, accessed October 1, 2014, http://www.dailymail.co.uk/news/article-2657724/Pope-Francis-claims-global-economy-close-collapse-describes-youth-unemployment-rates-atrocity-damning-message.html.
33. Steph Cockroft, "Pope Francis Claims Global Economy Is Close to Collapse and Describes Youth Unemployment Rates As an 'Atrocity' in Damning Message," *Daily Mail,* June 14, 2014, accessed October 1, 2014, http://www.dailymail.co.uk/news/article-2657724/Pope-Francis-claims-global-economy-close-collapse-describes-youth-unemployment-rates-atrocity-damning-message.html.
34. "CARA Frequently Requested Church Statistics," Georgetown University, accessed October 1, 2014, http://cara.georgetown.edu/caraservices/requestedchurchstats.html.
35. Todd G. Buchholz and Victoria Buchholz, "The Go-Nowhere Generation," *The New York Times*, March 10, 2012, accessed October 1, 2014, http://www.nytimes.com/2012/03/11/opinion/sunday/the-go-nowhere-generation.html?_r+=0&_r=0.
36. *Millennials in Adulthood,* Pew Research Center, accessed October 1, 2014, http://www.pewsocialtrends.org/2014/03/07/millennials-in-adulthood/.
37. Robert Rector, *Marriage: America's Greatest Weapon Against Child Poverty,* The Heritage Foundation, September 16, 2010, accessed October 1, 2014, http://www.heritage.org/research/reports/2010/09/marriage-america-s-greatest-weapon-against-child-poverty.
38. *Annual Poverty by Selected Characteristics 2009–2011*, "U.S. Census Bureau, accessed October 1, 2014, http://www.census.gov/hhes/www/poverty/publications/dynamics09/2b.pdf.
39. Robert Rector, "Marriage: America's Greatest Weapon Against Child Poverty," *The Heritage Foundation*, September 16, 2010, accessed October 1, 2014, http://www.heritage.org/research/reports/2010/09/marriage-america-s-greatest-weapon-against-child-poverty.
40. Annie Lowrey, "Can Marriage Cure Poverty?," *New York Times*, February 4, 2014, accessed October 1, 2014, http://www.nytimes.com/2014/02/09/magazine/can-marriage-cure-poverty.html.
41. *Millennials in Adulthood,* Pew Research Center, accessed October 1, 2014, http://www.pewsocialtrends.org/2014/03/07/millennials-in-adulthood/.

42. *Millennials in Adulthood,* Pew Research Center, accessed October 1, 2014, http://www.pewsocialtrends.org/2014/03/07/millennials-in-adulthood/.
43. Paul Bedard, "Harvard: Just 6 in 10 Millennials Have Jobs, Half Are Part-Time," *Washington Examiner,* February 7, 2013, accessed October 1, 2014, http://washingtonexaminer.com/harvard-just-6-in-10-millennials-have-jobs-half-are-part-time/article/2520719.
44. "December's Millennial Jobs Report: Youth Unemployment at 11.5 Percent," Generation Opportunity, accessed October 1, 2014, http://generationopportunity.org/press/decembers-millennial-jobs-report-youth-unemployment-at-11-5-percent/.
45. Meera Louis, "$1 Trillion Debt Crushes Business Dreams of U.S. Students," *Bloomberg,* June 6, 2013, accessed October 1, 2014, http://www.bloomberg.com/news/2013-06-06/-1-trillion-debt-crushes-business-dreams-of-u-s-students.html.
46. Elliot Blair Smith, "American Dream Fades for Generation Y Professionals," *Bloomberg,* December 21, 2012, accessed October 1, 2014, http://www.bloomberg.com/news/2012-12-21/american-dream-fades-for-generation-y-professionals.html.
47. Alfred Gottschalck and Marina Vornovytskyy, *Changes in Household Net Worth from 2005 to 2010,* U.S. Census Bureau, June 18, 2012, accessed October 1, 2014, http://blogs.census.gov/2012/06/18/changes-in-household-net-worth-from-2005-to-2010/.
48. *Millennials: The Politically Unclaimed Generation—The Reason-Rupe Spring 2014 Millennial Survey,* Reason Foundation, accessed October 1, 2014, http://reason.com/assets/db/2014-millennials-report.pdf.
49. "Millennials Think Government Is Inefficient, Abuses Its Power, and Supports Cronyism," Reason.com, accessed October 1, 2014, http://reason.com/poll/2014/07/10/reason-rupe-2014-millennial-survey.
50. "Millennials Think Government Is Inefficient, Abuses Its Power, and Supports Cronyism," Reason.com, accessed October 1, 2014, http://reason.com/poll/2014/07/10/reason-rupe-2014-millennial-survey.
51. "Millennial Support for Redistribution and Government Social Spending Declines with Income," Reason.com, accessed October 1, 2014, http://reason.com/blog/2014/07/10/millennial-support-for-redistribution-a2.
52. "Millennials Think Government Is Inefficient, Abuses Its Power, and Supports Cronyism," Reason.com, accessed October 1, 2014, http://reason.com/poll/2014/07/10/reason-rupe-2014-millennial-survey.

53. "Millennials Think Government Is Inefficient, Abuses Its Power, and Supports Cronyism," Reason.com, accessed October 1, 2014, http://reason.com/poll/2014/07/10/reason-rupe-2014-millennial-survey.
54. "Millennial Support for Redistribution and Government Social Spending Declines with Income," Reason.com, accessed October 1, 2014, http://reason.com/blog/2014/07/10/millennial-support-for-redistribution-a2.
55. "Millennial Support for Redistribution and Government Social Spending Declines with Income," Reason.com, accessed October 1, 2014, http://reason.com/blog/2014/07/10/millennial-support-for-redistribution-a2.
56. Michael Hais and Morley Winograd, "It's Official: Millennials Realigned American Politics in 2008," *Huffington Post*, December 18, 2008, accessed October 1, 2014, http://www.huffingtonpost.com/michael-hais-and-morley-winograd/its-official-millennials_b_144357.html.
57. "IOP Releases New Fall Poll, 5 Key Findings and Trends in Millennial Viewpoints," *Harvard University Institute of Politics Blog,* accessed October 1, 2014, http://iop.harvard.edu/blog/iop-releases-new-fall-poll-5-key-findings-and-trends-millennial-viewpoints?utm_source=homepage&utm_medium=hero&utm_campaign=Fall2013Survey.
58. "What's your Starbucks Signature?," *Starbucks Blog,* accessed October 1, 2014, http://www.starbucks.com/blog/what-s-your-starbucks-signature/674.
59. Post Editorial Board, "Free the Millennials!," *New York Post*, July 20, 2014, accessed October 1, 2014, http://nypost.com/2014/07/20/free-the-millennials/.
60. "*Millennials: The Politically Unclaimed Generation—The Reason-Rupe Spring 2014 Millennial Survey*, Reason Foundation, accessed October 1, 2014, http://reason.com/archives/2014/07/10/the-millennials-the-politically-unclaime.
61. Eric Liu, "Viewpoint: The Millennial Generation Can Lead Us Out of Gridlock," *Time,* March 12, 2013, accessed October 1, 2014, http://ideas.time.com/2013/03/12/viewpoint-the-millennial-generation-can-lead-us-out-of-gridlock/#comments.
62. "The American Dream Is Now Do-It-Yourself," MetLife, accessed October 1, 2014, https://www.metlife.com/about/press-room/index.html?compID=72458.
63. "The American Dream Is Now Do-It-Yourself," MetLife, accessed October 1, 2014, https://www.metlife.com/about/press-room/index.html?compID=72458.

64. "The American Dream Is Now Do-It-Yourself," MetLife, accessed October 1, 2014, https://www.metlife.com/about/press-room/index.html?compID=72458.
65. Andrea Coombes, "Boomers Blame Banks for Financial Crisis," *MarketWatch*, September 4, 2013, accessed October 1, 2014, http://www.marketwatch.com/story/boomers-blame-banks-for-financial-crisis-2013-09-04?pagenumber=1.
66. Morley Winograd and Michael Hais, "Millennials Lead the Nation in Service to Our Country," *NDN Blog*, August 19, 2009, accessed October 1, 2014, http://ndn.org/blog/2009/08/millennials-lead-nation-service-our-country.
67. Emily Ekins, *The Millennials: The Politically Unclaimed Generation*, Reason.com, accessed October 1, 2014, http://reason.com/archives/2014/07/10/the-millennials-the-politically-unclaime.
68. Emily Ekins, *The Millennials: The Politically Unclaimed Generation*, Reason.com, accessed October 1, 2014, http://reason.com/archives/2014/07/10/the-millennials-the-politically-unclaime.
69. *From the Margins to the Mainstream,* World Economic Forum, September 2013, accessed October 1, 2014, http://www3.weforum.org/docs/WEF_II_FromMarginsMainstream_Report_2013.pdf.
70. *The Millennial Survey 2014,* Deloitte, accessed October 1, 2014, http://www2.deloitte.com/global/en/pages/about-deloitte/articles/2014-millennial-survey-positive-impact.html.
71. David Madland and Ruy Teixeira, *New Progressive America: The Millennial Generation,* Center for American Progress, May 13, 2009, accessed October 1, 2014, http://www.americanprogress.org/issues/progressive-movement/report/2009/05/13/6133/new-progressive-america-the-millennial-generation/.
72. Jeanne Meister, "Three Reasons You Need to Adopt a Millennial Mindset Regardless of Your Age," *Forbes Online,* October 5, 2012, accessed October 1, 2014, http://www.forbes.com/sites/jeannemeister/2012/10/05/millennialmindse/.

## Chapter 3

1. Walter Isaacson, *The Innovators: How a Group of Inventors, Hackers, Geniuses, and Geeks Created the Digital Revolution* (New York: Simon & Schuster, 2014).
2. "Poverty Overview," World Bank, accessed October 1, 2014, http://www.worldbank.org/en/topic/poverty/overview.

3. "Poverty Overview," World Bank, accessed October 1, 2014, http://www.worldbank.org/en/topic/poverty/overview.
4. "Poverty Overview," World Bank, accessed October 1, 2014, http://www.worldbank.org/en/topic/poverty/overview.
5. Michael Tanner, "Capitalism's Triumph," *National Review Online*, September 18, 2013, accessed October 1, 2014, http://www.nationalreview.com/article/358771/capitalisms-triumph-michael-tanner.
6. "Hunger Vital Statistics," United Nations, accessed October 1, 2014, http://www.un.org/en/globalissues/briefingpapers/food/vitalstats.shtml
7. "Poverty Overview," World Bank, accessed October 1, 2014, http://www.worldbank.org/en/topic/poverty/overview.
8. Jacob Lundberg, "The Triumph of Global Capitalism," Adam Smith Institute, February 17, 2012, accessed October 1, 2014, http://www.adamsmith.org/research/think-pieces/the-triumph-of-global-capitalism/.
9. "Economic Freedom of the World," Cato Institute, accessed October 1, 2014, http://www.cato.org/economic-freedom-world.
10. "Economic Freedom of the World," Cato Institute, accessed October 1, 2014, http://www.cato.org/economic-freedom-world.
11. "Economic Freedom of the World," Cato Institute, accessed October 1, 2014, http://www.cato.org/economic-freedom-world.
12. Larry Elder, "Why Does Capitalism Still Need Defending?," Freedom Works, September 12, 2013, accessed October 1, 2014, http://connect.freedomworks.org/news/view/396320?destination=news.
13. Abraham Lincoln, "The Gettysburg Address" (speech given November 19, 1863, at the dedication of the cemetery at Gettysburg), accessed October 1, 2014, http://www.d.umn.edu/~rmaclin/gettysburg-address.html.
14. "The Gettysburg Address," History.com, accessed October 1, 2014, http://www.history.com/topics/american-civil-war/gettysburg-address.
15. George Clack, editor, *Abraham Lincoln: A Legacy of Freedom,* Bureau of International Information Programs, U.S. Department of State, accessed October 1, 2014, http://iipdigital.usembassy.gov/media/pdf/books/lincoln.pdf.
16. Christopher Fox Graham, "An Analysis of Abraham Lincoln's Poetic Gettysburg Address," *Fox the Poet Blog,* September 2008, accessed October 1, 2014, http://foxthepoet.blogspot.de/2008/09/poetical-analysis-of-abraham-lincolns.html.
17. "The Declaration of Independence," U.S. National Archives, accessed October 1, 2014, http://www.archives.gov/exhibits/charters/declaration_transcript.html.

18. Glenn Kessler, "The Facts About the Growth of Spending Under Obama," *Washington Post*, May 25, 2012, accessed October 1, 2014, http://www.washingtonpost.com/blogs/fact-checker/post/the-facts-about-the-growth-of-spending-under-obama/2012/05/24/gJQAIJh6nU_blog.html.
19. "An Analysis of the President's 2013 Budget," Congressional Budget Office, accessed October 1, 2014, http://www.cbo.gov/sites/default/files/cbofiles/attachments/03-16-APB1.pdf.
20. *Investopedia*, s.v. "Crowding Out Effect," accessed October 1, 2014, http://www.investopedia.com/terms/c/crowdingouteffect.asp.
21. David Greenlaw, James D. Hamilton, Peter Hooper, and Frederic S. Mishkin, *U.S. Monetary Policy Forum: Crunch Time Fiscal Crises and the Role of Monetary Policy* (paper written for the U.S. Monetary Policy Forum, New York City, February 22, 2013), delivered February 22, 2013, revised July 29, 2013, accessed October 1, 2014, http://research.chicagobooth.edu/igm/usmpf/download2.aspx.
22. Binyamin Appelbaum, "Predicting a Crisis, Repeatedly," *New York Times*, February 22, 2013, accessed October 1, 2014, http://economix.blogs.nytimes.com/2013/02/22/predicting-a-crisis-repeatedly/?_php=true&_type=blogs&_r=0.
23. Binyamin Appelbaum, "Predicting a Crisis, Repeatedly," *New York Times*, February 22, 2013, accessed October 1, 2014, http://economix.blogs.nytimes.com/2013/02/22/predicting-a-crisis-repeatedly/?_php=true&_type=blogs&_r=0.
24. Binyamin Appelbaum, "Predicting a Crisis, Repeatedly," *New York Times*, February 22, 2013, accessed October 1, 2014, http://economix.blogs.nytimes.com/2013/02/22/predicting-a-crisis-repeatedly/?_php=true&_type=blogs&_r=0.
25. David Greenlaw, James D. Hamilton, Peter Hooper, and Frederic S. Mishkin, *U.S. Monetary Policy Forum: Crunch Time Fiscal Crises and the Role of Monetary Policy,* (paper written for the U.S. Monetary Policy Forum, New York City, February 22, 2013), delivered February 22, 2013, revised July 29, 2013, February 22, 2013, accessed October 1, 2014, http://research.chicagobooth.edu/igm/usmpf/download2.aspx.
26. David Greenlaw, James D. Hamilton, Peter Hooper, and Frederic S. Mishkin, *U.S. Monetary Policy Forum: Crunch Time Fiscal Crises and the Role of Monetary Policy,* (paper written for the U.S. Monetary Policy Forum, New York City, February 22, 2013), delivered February 22, 2013, revised July 29, 2013, February 22, 2013,

accessed October 1, 2014, http://research.chicagobooth.edu/igm/usmpf/download2.aspx.

27. Binyamin Appelbaum, "Predicting a Crisis, Repeatedly," *New York Times*, February 22, 2013, accessed October 1, 2014, http://economix.blogs.nytimes.com/2013/02/22/predicting-a-crisis-repeatedly/?_php=true&_type=blogs&_r=0.
28. Michael Tanner, "Capitalism's Triumph," *National Review Online*, September 18, 2013, accessed October 1, 2014, http://www.nationalreview.com/article/358771/capitalisms-triumph-michael-tanner.
29. "Deng Xiaoping," Reference.com, accessed October 1, 2014, http://www.reference.com/browse/deng+xiaoping.
30. Evan Osnos, "To Get Rich Is Glorious," *New Yorker,* December 7, 2009, accessed October 1, 2014, http://www.newyorker.com/news/evan-osnos/to-get-rich-is-glorious.
31. Henrik Edberg, "What Confucius Can Teach You About Living a Happier Life," *The Positivity Blog*, accessed October 1, 2014, http://www.positivityblog.com/index.php/2010/07/07/what-confucius-can-teach-you-about-living-a-happier-life/.
32. *Encyclopedia of Contemporary Chinese Culture,* s.v. "New Confucianism," accessed October 1, 2014, http://contemporary_chinese_culture.academic.ru/556/New_Confucianism.
33. "The Declaration of Independence," U.S. National Archives, accessed October 1, 2014, http://www.archives.gov/exhibits/charters/declaration_transcript.html.
34. "China's Government May Be Communist, but Its People Embrace Capitalism," Pew Research Center, accessed October 10, 2014, http://www.pewresearch.org/fact-tank/2014/10/10/chinas-government-may-be-communist-but-its-people-embrace-capitalism/.
35. "China's Government May Be Communist, but Its People Embrace Capitalism," Pew Research Center, accessed October 10, 2014, http://www.pewresearch.org/fact-tank/2014/10/10/chinas-government-may-be-communist-but-its-people-embrace-capitalism/.
36. Charles Murray, "Why Capitalism Has an Image Problem," *Wall Street Journal,* July 30, 2012, accessed October 1, 2014, http://online.wsj.com/news/articles/SB10000872396390443931404577549223178294822?mod=googlenews_wsj&mg=reno64-wsj&url=http%3A%2F%2Fonline.wsj.com%2Farticle%2FSB10000872396390443931404577549223178294822.html%3Fmod%3Dgooglenews_wsj.

37. Charles Murray, "Why Capitalism Has an Image Problem," *Wall Street Journal,* July 30, 2012, accessed October 1, 2014, http://online.wsj.com/news/articles/SB10000872396390443931404577549223178294822?mod=googlenews_wsj&mg=reno64-wsj&url=http%3A%2F%2Fonline.wsj.com%2Farticle%2FSB10000872396390443931404577549223178294822.html%3Fmod%3Dgooglenews_wsj.
38. Jessica Guynn, "Airbnb Looks to Rally Support as Regulators Scrutinize Business," *Los Angeles Times*, November 12, 2013, accessed October 1, 2014, http://articles.latimes.com/2013/nov/12/business/la-fi-tn-airbnb-looks-to-rally-support-as-regulators-scrutinize-business-20131112.
39. Jessica Guynn, "Airbnb Looks to Rally Support as Regulators Scrutinize Business," *Los Angeles Times*, November 12, 2013, accessed October 1, 2014, http://articles.latimes.com/2013/nov/12/business/la-fi-tn-airbnb-looks-to-rally-support-as-regulators-scrutinize-business-20131112.
40. *Wikipedia,* s.v. "Brian Chesky," accessed October 1, 2014, http://en.wikipedia.org/wiki/Brian_Chesky.
41. Jessica Guynn, "Airbnb Looks to Rally Support as Regulators Scrutinize Business," *Los Angeles Times*, November 12, 2013, accessed October 1, 2014, http://articles.latimes.com/2013/nov/12/business/la-fi-tn-airbnb-looks-to-rally-support-as-regulators-scrutinize-business-20131112.
42. "OECD Data," Organisation for Economic Co-operation and Development," accessed October 1, 2014, http://www.oecd.org/statistics/.
43. Brian Roach, *Corporate Power in a Global Economy,* Tufts University Global Development and Environment Institute, accessed October 1, 2014, http://www.ase.tufts.edu/Gdae/education_materials/modules/Corporate_Power_in_a_Global_Economy.pdf.
44. "Apple Inc. (AAPL)," Yahoo Finance, accessed April 30, 2014, http://finance.yahoo.com/q?s=AAPL.
45. "Microsoft Corporation (MSFT)," Yahoo Finance, accessed April 30, 2014, http://finance.yahoo.com/q?s=MSFT.
46. Sophie Murray-Morris, "Apple and Microsoft Have Bigger Cash Holdings than UK," *Telegraph* (U.K.), April 11, 2014, accessed October 1, 2014, http://www.telegraph.co.uk/finance/businesslatestnews/10760392/Apple-and-Microsoft-have-bigger-cash-holdings-than-UK.html.
47. Tim Worstall, "Fun Number; Apple Has Twice as Much Cash as the U.S. Government," *Forbes Online*, April 13, 2014, accessed October 1,

2014, http://www.forbes.com/sites/timworstall/2014/04/13/fun-number-apple-has-twice-as-much-cash-as-the-us-government/.

48. Rik Myslewski, "Apple Has Three Times as Much Cash as U.S. Government, Twice the UK," *Register* (U.K.), April 11, 2014, accessed October 1, 2014, http://www.theregister.co.uk/2014/04/11/apple_has_three_times_as_much_cash_as_us_govt_twice_the_uk/.
49. "Why We Need Health Care Reform," Obamacare Facts, accessed October 1, 2014, http://obamacarefacts.com/healthcare-facts.php.
50. "Corporate Locations," Walmart Corporation, accessed October 1, 2014, http://corporate.walmart.com/our-story/locations/united-states.
51. Dan Diamond, "Walmart Announces Ambitious Goal: 'To Be the Number One Healthcare Provider in the Industry," *Forbes Online*, October 6, 2014, accessed October 6, 2014, http://www.forbes.com/sites/dandiamond/2014/10/06/walmart-announces-ambitious-goal-to-be-the-number-one-healthcare-provider/.
52. Dan Diamond, "Walmart Announces Ambitious Goal: 'To Be the Number One Healthcare Provider in the Industry," *Forbes Online*, October 6, 2014, accessed October 6, 2014, http://www.forbes.com/sites/dandiamond/2014/10/06/walmart-announces-ambitious-goal-to-be-the-number-one-healthcare-provider/.
53. Dan Diamond, "Walmart Announces Ambitious Goal: 'To Be the Number One Healthcare Provider in the Industry'," *Forbes Online,* October 6, 2014, accessed October 6, 2014, http://www.forbes.com/sites/dandiamond/2014/10/06/walmart-announces-ambitious-goal-to-be-the-number-one-healthcare-provider/.
54. Richard Pollock, "Surprise! Walmart Health Plan Is Cheaper, Offers More Coverage than Obamacare," *Washington Examiner*, January 7, 2014, accessed October 1, 2014, http://washingtonexaminer.com/surprise-walmart-health-plan-is-cheaper-offers-more-coverage-than-obamacare/article/2541670.
55. Elliot Smilowitz, "Infographic: Obamacare vs. Walmart, Premium Comparison," *Washington Examiner,* January 7, 2014, accessed October 1, 2014, http://washingtonexaminer.com/article/2541665.
56. *Wikipedia,* s.v. "Earth Summit," accessed October 1, 2014, http://en.wikipedia.org/wiki/Earth_Summit.
57. "Starbucks Global Responsibility Report: Goals and Progress 2013," Starbucks Corporation, accessed October 1, 2014, http://globalassets.starbucks.com/assets/98e5a8e6c7b1435ab67f2368b1c7447a.pdf.

58. Editorial Board, "Minimum Wage Hike Imperils Chicago Job Creation," *Chicago Tribune,* July 16, 2014, accessed October 1, 2014, http://www.chicagotribune.com/news/opinion/editorials/ct-minimum-wage-chicago-edit-0716-20140716-story.html.
59. John Carney, "Lloyd Blankfein Says He Is Doing 'God's Work,'" *Business Insider,* November 9, 2009, accessed October 1, 2014, http://www.businessinsider.com.au/lloyd-blankfein-says-he-is-doing-gods-work-2009-11.
60. Matt Phillips, "Goldman Sachs' Blankfein on Banking Doing 'God's Work,'" *Wall Street Journal,* November 9, 2009, accessed October 1, 2014, http://blogs.wsj.com/marketbeat/2009/11/09/goldman-sachs-blankfein-on-banking-doing-gods-work/.

## Chapter 4

1. Larry J. Sechrest, "Explaining Malinvestment and Overinvestment," Sul Ross State University, October 2005, accessed October 1, 2014, https://mises.org/journals/scholar/Sechrest10.pdf.
2. "Impact Investing: Judith Rodin Takes On the Naysayers," Knowledge @ Wharton, University of Pennsylvania, June 9, 2014, accessed October 1, 2014, http://knowledge.wharton.upenn.edu/article/putting-markets-work-profit-global-good/.
3. Antony Bugg-Levine and Jed Emerson, *Impact Investing: Transforming How We Make Money While Making a Difference,* (San Francisco: Jossey-Bass, 2011).
4. *Wikipedia,* s.v. "Alejandro Jodorowsky," accessed October 1, 2014, http://en.wikipedia.org/wiki/Alejandro_Jodorowsky.
5. *Wikipedia,* s.v. "Warren Buffett," accessed October 1, 2014, http://en.wikipedia.org/wiki/Warren_Buffett.
6. *From the Margins to the Mainstream,* World Economic Forum, September 2013, accessed October 1, 2014, http://www3.weforum.org/docs/WEF_II_FromMarginsMainstream_Report_2013.pdf.
7. "S&P 500 Companies with Financial Information," Data OKFN, accessed October 1, 2014, http://data.okfn.org/data/core/s-and-p-500-companies.
8. "2014 Berkshire Hathaway Annual Q&A with Warren Buffett and Charlie Munger," The Motley Fool, May 21, 2014, accessed October 1, 2014, http://www.fool.com/investing/general/2014/05/21/2014-berkshire-hathaway-annual-qa-with-warren-buff.aspx.

9. Kelly Phillips Erb, "Registration for Warren Buffett's $1 Billion Basketball Challenge Opens Today," *Forbes Online*, March 3, 2014, accessed October 1, 2014, http://www.forbes.com/sites/kellyphillipserb/2014/03/03/registration-for-warren-buffetts-1-billion-basketball-challenge-opens-today/.
10. Andy Kiersz, "Actually, the Odds Of Winning Warren Buffett's Billion Dollar Bracket Challenge Are Way Better than 1 in 9,223,372,036,854,775,808," *Business Insider*, January 22, 2014, accessed October 1, 2014, http://www.businessinsider.com/odds-of-perfect-ncaa-buffett-bracket-2014-1#ixzz3FlIqDNXL.
11. Noah Rayman, "No One Won Warren Buffett's $1 Billion Bracket Challenge," *Time* magazine, March 22, 2014, accessed October 1, 2014, http://time.com/34358/no-one-won-warren-buffetts-1-billion-bracket-challenge/.
12. Janet Lowe, *Warren Buffett Speaks: Wit and Wisdom from the World's Greatest Investor,* (New York: Wiley, 2007).
13. "Impact Bonds," Social Finance Ltd., accessed October 1, 2014, http://www.socialfinance.org.uk/services/social-impact-bonds/.
14. *2013–2014 State of the Schools Report,* Nebraska Department of Education, accessed October 1, 2014, http://reportcard.education.ne.gov/.
15. *Investing with Impact*, Morgan Stanley, accessed October 1, 2014, http://www.morganstanley.com/globalcitizen/pdf/investing-with-impact.pdf?v=07112013.
16. *From the Margins to the Mainstream*, World Economic Forum, September 2013, accessed October 1, 2014, http://www3.weforum.org/docs/WEF_II_FromMarginsMainstream_Report_2013.pdf.
17. *Investing for Social & Environmental Impact,* Monitor Institute: January 2009, accessed October 1, 2014, http://monitorinstitute.com/downloads/what-we-think/impact-investing/Impact_Investing.pdf.
18. Jeremy K. Balkin, "The Noble Cause: Positively Influencing the Allocation of Capital," TEDxColumbiaEngineering, October 25, 2013, accessed October 1, 2014, https://www.youtube.com/watch?v=rXyRlfI8Tvo.
19. Jeremy K. Balkin, "Values in Business," UNSW Business School, February 25, 2014, accessed October 1, 2014, https://www.youtube.com/watch?v=rXyRlfI8Tvo. http://youtu.be/-G2Gyuzp1Kg.
20. Jeremy K. Balkin, "The Noble Cause: Positively Influencing the Allocation of Capital," TEDxColumbiaEngineering, October 25, 2013, accessed October 1, 2014, https://www.youtube.com/watch?v=rXyRlfI8Tvo.

21. *Investopedia,* s.v. "Socially Responsible Investment—SRI," accessed October 1, 2014, http://www.investopedia.com/terms/s/sri.asp.
22. *Investopedia,* s.v. "Environmental, Social and Governance (ESG) Criteria," accessed October 1, 2014, http://www.investopedia.com/terms/e/environmental-social-and-governance-esg-criteria.asp.
23. *Investopedia,* "Definition of Ethical Investing," accessed October 1, 2014, http://www.investopedia.com/terms/e/ethical-investing.asp.
24. *Global Pension Assets Study 2014,* Towers Watson, January 2014, accessed October 1, 2014, http://conferences.pionline.com/assets/2014_GPAS_Study_Final.pdf.
25. *From the Margins to the Mainstream,* World Economic Forum: September 2013, accessed October 1, 2014, http://www3.weforum.org/docs/WEF_II_FromMarginsMainstream_Report_2013.pdf.
26. *The Millennial Survey 2014,* Deloitte, accessed October 1, 2014, http://www2.deloitte.com/global/en/pages/about-deloitte/articles/2014-millennial-survey-positive-impact.html.
27. *The Millennial Survey 2014,* Deloitte, accessed October 1, 2014, http://www2.deloitte.com/global/en/pages/about-deloitte/articles/2014-millennial-survey-positive-impact.html.
28. David Wessel, "Fewer New Harvard Grads Head to Wall Street, Consulting," *Wall Street Journal*, June 4, 2009, accessed October 1, 2014, http://blogs.wsj.com/economics/2009/06/04/fewer-new-harvard-grads-head-to-wall-street-consulting/.
29. Naveen N. Srivatsa, "Harvard Seniors Headed to Workforce Holds Steady," *Harvard Crimson*, May 22, 2012, accessed October 1, 2014, http://www.thecrimson.com/article/2012/5/22/senior-survey-commencement-naveen/.
30. Robert Rubinstein, "Millennial Recruitment and Impact Investing," *Huffington Post*, August 19, 2014, accessed October 1, 2014, http://www.huffingtonpost.com/robert-rubinstein/millennial-recruitment-impact-investing_b_5691544.html?utm_hp_ref=business&ir=Business.
31. Robert Rubinstein, "Millennial Recruitment and Impact Investing," *Huffington Post*, August 19, 2014, accessed October 1, 2014, http://www.huffingtonpost.com/robert-rubinstein/millennial-recruitment-impact-investing_b_5691544.html?utm_hp_ref=business&ir=Business.
32. Robert Rubinstein, "Millennial Recruitment and Impact Investing," *Huffington Post*, August 19, 2014, accessed October 1, 2014, http://www.huffingtonpost.com/robert-rubinstein/millennial-recruitment

-impact-investing_b_5691544.html?utm_hp_ref=business&ir=Business.
33. Jeremy K. Balkin, "The Noble Cause: Positively Influencing the Allocation of Capital," TEDxColumbiaEngineering October 25, 2013, accessed October 1, 2014, https://www.youtube.com/watch?v=rXyRlfI8Tvo.
34. *The Millennial Survey 2014,* Deloitte, accessed October 1, 2014, http://www2.deloitte.com/global/en/pages/about-deloitte/articles/2014-millennial-survey-positive-impact.html.
35. *The Millennial Survey 2014,* Deloitte, accessed October 1, 2014, http://www2.deloitte.com/global/en/pages/about-deloitte/articles/2014-millennial-survey-positive-impact.html.
36. *The Millennial Survey 2014,* Deloitte, accessed October 1, 2014, http://www2.deloitte.com/global/en/pages/about-deloitte/articles/2014-millennial-survey-positive-impact.html.
37. *The Millennial Survey 2014,* Deloitte, accessed October 1, 2014, http://www2.deloitte.com/global/en/pages/about-deloitte/articles/2014-millennial-survey-positive-impact.html.
38. *The Millennial Survey 2014,* Deloitte, accessed October 1, 2014, http://www2.deloitte.com/global/en/pages/about-deloitte/articles/2014-millennial-survey-positive-impact.html.
39. *The Millennial Survey 2014,* Deloitte, accessed October 1, 2014, http://www2.deloitte.com/global/en/pages/about-deloitte/articles/2014-millennial-survey-positive-impact.html.
40. *The Millennial Survey 2014,* Deloitte, accessed October 1, 2014, http://www2.deloitte.com/global/en/pages/about-deloitte/articles/2014-millennial-survey-positive-impact.html.
41. *The Millennial Survey 2014,* Deloitte, accessed October 1, 2014, http://www2.deloitte.com/global/en/pages/about-deloitte/articles/2014-millennial-survey-positive-impact.html.
42. *Global Pension Assets Study 2014,* Towers Watson January 2014, accessed October 1, 2014, http://conferences.pionline.com/assets/2014_GPAS_Study_Final.pdf.
43. "Morgan Stanley Smith Barney Announces Launch of Investing with Impact Platform," Morgan Stanley, April 26, 2012, accessed October 1, 2014, http://www.morganstanley.com/about/press/articles/8d25155d-790c-4926-be23-dd559696b3b7.html.
44. "Starbucks Investor Relations," Starbucks Corporation, accessed October 1, 2014, http://investor.starbucks.com/phoenix.zhtml?c=99518&p

=irol-stocklookup&t=HistQuote&submit.x=76&submit.y=20&submit =Look%20Up&control_firstdatereturned=.

## Chapter 5

1. "Warren Buffett: Beware of 'Impact Investing,'" *Forbes Online*, accessed October 1, 2014, http://www.forbes.com/video/2886856992001/.
2. Anne Field, "Biggest 'Social Impact Bond' in the U.S. Targets Recidivism," *Forbes Online,* February 7, 2014, accessed October 1, 2014, http://www.forbes.com/sites/annefield/2014/02/07/biggest-social-impact-bond-in-the-u-s-targets-stubborn-recidivism/.
3. Antony Bugg-Levine and Jed Emerson, *Impact Investing: Transforming How We Make Money While Making a Difference* (San Francisco: Jossey-Bass, 2011).
4. Antony Bugg-Levine and Jed Emerson, *Impact Investing: Transforming How We Make Money While Making a Difference* (San Francisco: Jossey-Bass, 2011).
5. *Global Pension Assets Study 2014,* Towers Watson, January 2014, accessed October 1, 2014, http://conferences.pionline.com/assets/2014_GPAS_Study_Final.pdf.
6. Wayne M. Morrison, *China's Economic Rise: History, Trends, Challenges, and Implications for the United States,* Congressional Research Service, October 9, 2014, accessed October 30, 2014, https://www.fas.org/sgp/crs/row/RL33534.pdf.
7. "Data & Statistics," International Monetary Fund, accessed October 1, 2014, http://www.imf.org/external/data.htm.
8. Malcolm Maiden, "BHP Is Not Only Leaner, It's Greener," *Sydney Morning Herald*, September 25, 2014, accessed October 1, 2014, http://www.smh.com.au/business/comment-and-analysis/bhp-is-not-only-leaner-its-greener-20140925-10lwdu.html#ixzz3G2MG62Cj.
9. Malcolm Maiden, "BHP Is Not Only Leaner, It's Greener," *Sydney Morning Herald*, September 25, 2014, accessed October 1, 2014, http://www.smh.com.au/business/comment-and-analysis/bhp-is-not-only-leaner-its-greener-20140925-10lwdu.html#ixzz3G2MG62Cj.
10. Malcolm Maiden, "BHP Is Not Only Leaner, It's Greener," *Sydney Morning Herald*, September 25, 2014, accessed October 1, 2014, http://www.smh.com.au/business/comment-and-analysis/bhp-is-not-only-leaner-its-greener-20140925-10lwdu.html#ixzz3G2MG62Cj.

11. Malcolm Maiden, "BHP Is Not Only Leaner, It's Greener," *Sydney Morning Herald*, September 25, 2014, accessed October 1, 2014, http://www.smh.com.au/business/comment-and-analysis/bhp-is-not-only-leaner-its-greener-20140925-10lwdu.html#ixzz3G2MG62Cj.
12. N. Gregory Mankiw, *Macroeconomics* (New York: Worth Publishers, 2003), 167.
13. Mark Muro, "Multiplier Effects: Connecting the Innovation and Opportunity Agendas," *Brookings Blog,* August 23, 2012, accessed October 1, 2014, http://www.brookings.edu/blogs/the-avenue/posts/2012/08/23-multiplier-effects-muro.
14. William Alden, "Wall Street's Young Bankers Are Still Mostly White and Male, Report Says," *New York Times,* September 30, 2014, accessed October 1, 2014, http://dealbook.nytimes.com/2014/09/30/wall-streets-young-bankers-are-still-mostly-white-and-male/.
15. *IMDB,* s.v. "The Wolf of Wall Street," accessed October 1, 2014, http://www.imdb.com/title/tt0993846/.
16. Jessica Grose, "Are Wall Street Banks Still Dumb Enough to Hold Meetings in Strip Clubs?" *Slate*, July 3, 2014, accessed October 1, 2014, http://www.slate.com/blogs/xx_factor/2014/07/03/goldman_sachs_discrimination_suit_lawsuit_alleges_sexism_strip_club_meetings.html.
17. Benjamin Goad, "Feds to Track Diversity at Wall Street Banks," *The Hill*, October 24, 2013, accessed October 1 2014, http://thehill.com/regulation/finance/186391-feds-track-diversity-wall-street-banks.
18. Thomas Barta, Markus Kleiner, and Tilo Neumann, "Is There a Payoff from Top-Team Diversity?," *McKinsey Quarterly*, April 2012, accessed October 1, 2014, http://www.mckinsey.com/insights/organization/is_there_a_payoff_from_top-team_diversity.
19. Thomas Barta, Markus Kleiner, and Tilo Neumann, "Is There a Payoff from Top-Team Diversity?," *McKinsey Quarterly*, April 2012, accessed October 1, 2014, http://www.mckinsey.com/insights/organization/is_there_a_payoff_from_top-team_diversity.
20. Thomas Barta, Markus Kleiner, and Tilo Neumann, "Is There a Payoff from Top-Team Diversity?," *McKinsey Quarterly*, April 2012, accessed October 1, 2014, http://www.mckinsey.com/insights/organization/is_there_a_payoff_from_top-team_diversity.
21. "FINRA Administered Qualification Examinations," Financial Industry Regulatory Authority (FINRA), accessed October 1, 2014, http://

www.finra.org/industry/compliance/registration/qualificationsexams/qualifications/p011096.

22. "The Growing Economic Clout of the College Educated," *Fact-Tank Blog*, Pew Research Center, accessed October 1, 2014, http://www.pewresearch.org/fact-tank/2013/09/24/the-growing-economic-clout-of-the-college-educated/.
23. Ken Silverstein, "Enron, Ethics and Today's Corporate Values," *Forbes Online*, May 14, 2014, accessed October 1, 2014, http://www.forbes.com/sites/kensilverstein/2013/05/14/enron-ethics-and-todays-corporate-values/.
24. Ken Silverstein, "Enron, Ethics and Today's Corporate Values," *Forbes Online*, May 14, 2014, accessed October 1, 2014, http://www.forbes.com/sites/kensilverstein/2013/05/14/enron-ethics-and-todays-corporate-values/.
25. Ken Silverstein, "Enron, Ethics and Today's Corporate Values," *Forbes Online*, May 14, 2014, accessed October 1, 2014, http://www.forbes.com/sites/kensilverstein/2013/05/14/enron-ethics-and-todays-corporate-values/.
26. Ken Silverstein, "Enron, Ethics and Today's Corporate Values," *Forbes Online*, May 14, 2014, accessed October 1, 2014, http://www.forbes.com/sites/kensilverstein/2013/05/14/enron-ethics-and-todays-corporate-values/.
27. Ken Silverstein, "Enron, Ethics and Today's Corporate Values," *Forbes Online*, May 14, 2014, accessed October 1, 2014, http://www.forbes.com/sites/kensilverstein/2013/05/14/enron-ethics-and-todays-corporate-values/.
28. Robert Lenzner, "Bernie Madoff's $50 Billion Ponzi Scheme," *Forbes Online*, December 12, 2008, accessed October 1, 2014, http://www.forbes.com/2008/12/12/madoff-ponzi-hedge-pf-ii-in_rl_1212croesus_inl.html.
29. Robert Lenzner, "Bernie Madoff's $50 Billion Ponzi Scheme," *Forbes Online*, December 12, 2008, accessed October 1, 2014, http://www.forbes.com/2008/12/12/madoff-ponzi-hedge-pf-ii-in_rl_1212croesus_inl.html.
30. Stephanie Strom, "Elie Wiesel Levels Scorn at Madoff," *New York Times*, February 26, 2009, accessed October 1, 2014, http://www.nytimes.com/2009/02/27/business/27madoff.html?_r=0.
31. Daniel Fisher, "SEC's Secret $30 Million Whistleblower Case Won't Improve Corporate Behavior," *Forbes Online*, September 25, 2014, accessed October 1, 2014, http://www.forbes.com/sites/danielfisher/2014/09/25/secs-secret-30-million-whistleblower-case-wont-improve-corporate-behavior/.
32. Robert G. Eccles, Ioannis Ioannou, and George Serafeim, *The Impact of a Corporate Culture of Sustainability on Corporate Behavior and Performance* (working paper), Harvard Business School, May 9,

2012, accessed October 1, 2014, http://cgt.columbia.edu/wp-content/uploads/2013/12/Corporate_culture_of_Sustainability.pdf.

33. Robert G. Eccles, Ioannis Ioannou, and George Serafeim, *The Impact of a Corporate Culture of Sustainability on Corporate Behavior and Performance* (working paper), Harvard Business School, May 9, 2012, accessed October 1, 2014, http://cgt.columbia.edu/wp-content/uploads/2013/12/Corporate_culture_of_Sustainability.pdf.
34. Robert G. Eccles, Ioannis Ioannou, and George Serafeim, *The Impact of a Corporate Culture of Sustainability on Corporate Behavior and Performance* (working paper), Harvard Business School, May 9, 2012, accessed October 1, 2014, http://cgt.columbia.edu/wp-content/uploads/2013/12/Corporate_culture_of_Sustainability.pdf.
35. Robert G. Eccles, Ioannis Ioannou, and George Serafeim, *The Impact of a Corporate Culture of Sustainability on Corporate Behavior and Performance* (working paper), Harvard Business School, May 9, 2012, accessed October 1, 2014, http://cgt.columbia.edu/wp-content/uploads/2013/12/Corporate_culture_of_Sustainability.pdf.
36. "Environmental, Social, and Governance (ESG) Reporting Requirements," ESG Analytics, accessed October 1, 2014, http://esganalytics.com/esg-reporting-requirements/.
37. "Starbucks: What's Your Starbucks Signature?," Starbucks Corporation, accessed October 1, 2014, http://www.starbucks.com/blog/what-s-your-starbucks-signature/674.
38. Brainyquote.com, s.v. "Howard Schultz Quotes," accessed October 1, 2014, http://www.brainyquote.com/quotes/authors/h/howard_schultz.html#6JtBX7zsTVy6HdA0.99.
39. Joel Coen, "Starbucks Paying for College—Conscious Capitalism?," *Investment You Blog,* accessed October 1, 2014, http://investmentyou.org/tag/conscious-capitalism/.
40. "Starbucks Corporation. (SBUX)," Yahoo Finance, accessed August 30, 2014, http://finance.yahoo.com/q?s=SBUX.
41. Ted Cooper, "6 Facts About Starbucks That Will Blow Your Mind," The Motley Fool, November 24, 2013, accessed October 1, 2014, http://www.fool.com/investing/general/2013/11/24/6-facts-about-starbucks-that-will-blow-your-mind.aspx.
42. "Joel Coen, "Starbucks Paying for College—Conscious Capitalism?," *Investment You Blog,* accessed October 1, 2014, http://investmentyou.org/tag/conscious-capitalism/.

43. Brainyquote.com, s.v. "Howard Schultz Quotes," accessed October 1, 2014, http://www.brainyquote.com/quotes/authors/h/howard_schultz.html#6JtBX7zsTVy6HdA0.99.
44. Brainyquote.com, s.v. "Howard Schultz Quotes," accessed October 1, 2014, http://www.brainyquote.com/quotes/authors/h/howard_schultz.html#6JtBX7zsTVy6HdA0.99.
45. "Global Responsibility Report: Goals and Progress 2013," Starbucks Corporation, accessed October 1, 2014, http://globalassets.starbucks.com/assets/98e5a8e6c7b1435ab67f2368b1c7447a.pdf.
46. "Starbucks: Working at Starbucks," Starbucks Corporation, accessed October 1, 2014, http://www.starbucks.com/careers/working-at-starbucks.
47. Brainyquote.com, s.v. "Howard Schultz Quotes," accessed October 1, 2014, http://www.brainyquote.com/quotes/authors/h/howard_schultz.html#6JtBX7zsTVy6HdA0.99.
48. "Starbucks: Working at Starbucks," Starbucks Corporation, accessed October 1, 2014, http://www.starbucks.com/careers/working-at-starbucks.
49. "Leading with Diversity," *New York Times*, accessed October 1, 2014, http://www.nytimes.com/marketing/jobmarket/diversity/starbucks.html.
50. Ulla P. Morais, Bahaudin G. Mujtaba, Jacqueline Pena, Yesenia Rivera, Roiner Ruiz, Kevin Shacket, and Lucien Sintilus, "Managing Diverse Employees at Starbucks: Focusing on Ethics and Inclusion," International Journal of Learning and Development, 2014, Vol. 4, No. 3, Doi:10.5296/ijld.v4i3.5994, accessed October 1, 2014, www.macrothink.org/journal/index.php/ijld/article/download/5994/4836.
51. "Global Responsibility Report: Goals and Progress 2013," Starbucks Corporation, accessed October 1, 2014, http://globalassets.starbucks.com/assets/98e5a8e6c7b1435ab67f2368b1c7447a.pdf.
52. "Global Responsibility Report: Goals and Progress 2013," Starbucks Corporation, accessed October 1, 2014, http://globalassets.starbucks.com/assets/98e5a8e6c7b1435ab67f2368b1c7447a.pdf.
53. "College Plan," Starbucks Corporation, accessed October 1, 2014, http://www.starbucks.com/careers/college-plan.
54. International Coffee Organization, accessed October 1, 2014, http://www.ico.org/.
55. "Global Responsibility Report: Goals and Progress 2013," Starbucks Corporation, accessed October 1, 2014, http://globalassets.starbucks.com/assets/98e5a8e6c7b1435ab67f2368b1c7447a.pdf.

56. "Global Responsibility Report: Goals and Progress 2013," Starbucks Corporation, accessed October 1, 2014, http://globalassets.starbucks.com/assets/98e5a8e6c7b1435ab67f2368b1c7447a.pdf.
57. "Global Responsibility Report: Goals and Progress 2013," Starbucks Corporation, accessed October 1, 2014, http://globalassets.starbucks.com/assets/98e5a8e6c7b1435ab67f2368b1c7447a.pdf.
58. "Goals & Progress: Cup Recycling," Starbucks Corporation, accessed October 1, 2014, http://www.starbucks.com/responsibility/global-report/environmental-stewardship/cup-recycling.
59. "Goals & Progress: Goals & Progress: Water Conservation," Starbucks Corporation, accessed October 1, 2014, http://www.starbucks.com/responsibility/global-report/environmental-stewardship/water-conservation.
60. "Vanguard Total Stock Market Index Fund Investor Shares (VTSMX)," CNN Money, accessed October 1, 2014, http://money.cnn.com/quote/mutualfund/mutualfund.html?symb=VTSMX.

## Chapter 6

1. *Global Pension Assets Study 2014,* Towers Watson, January 2014, accessed October 1, 2014, http://conferences.pionline.com/assets/2014_GPAS_Study_Final.pdf.
2. "Who Are the Unbanked?," Citi FT Financial Education Summit 2014 site, accessed October 1, 2014, http://event.ft-live.com/ehome/finedu2014/unbankedInfographic/?&.
3. "World Population Public Data," Google, accessed October 1, 2014, https://www.google.com/publicdata/explore?ds=d5bncppjof8f9_&met_y=sp_pop_totl&hl=en&dl=en.
4. "Who Are the Unbanked?," Citi FT Financial Education Summit 2014 site, accessed October 1, 2014, http://event.ft-live.com/ehome/finedu2014/unbankedInfographic/?&.
5. Dev Kar and Brian LeBlanc, *Illicit Financial Flows from Developing Countries: 2002–2011,* Global Financial Integrity, December 2013, accessed October 1, 2014, http://iff.gfintegrity.org/iff2013/Illicit_Financial_Flows_from_Developing_Countries_2002-2011-HighRes.pdf.
6. Bjørn Lomborg, "Dirty Development Money," Project Syndicate, accessed October 14, 2014, http://www.project-syndicate.org/commentary/illicit-financial-flows-and-the-post-2015-development-agenda-by-bj-rn-lomborg-2014-10#sTBURdp4fr81vcJq.99.

7. “Awards & Recognition,” Grameen Foundation, accessed October 1, 2014, http://www.grameenfoundation.org/about/awards-recognition.
8. Keith Bradsher and Anand Giridharadas, “Microloan Pioneer and His Bank Win Nobel Peace Prize,” *New York Times,* October 13, 2006, accessed October 1, 2014, http://www.nytimes.com/2006/10/13/business/14nobelcnd.html.
9. “Profit and Loss Account,” Grameen Bank, accessed October 1, 2014, http://www.grameen-info.org/index.php?option=com_content&task=view&id=1069&Itemid=937.
10. Virginia Tan, *“Microinsurance,”* Allen & Overy LLP, June 2012, accessed October 2014, http://a4id.org/sites/default/files/files/Short%20guide%20to%20Microinsurance.pdf.
11. “Library,” Alliance for Financial Inclusion, accessed October 1, 2014, http://www.afi-global.org/library.
12. Andrew Cave, “Banking for the Poor: Will This Be Bill Gates’ Greatest Philanthropic Achievement?,” *Forbes Online*, July 31, 2014, accessed October 1, 2014, http://www.forbes.com/sites/andrewcave/2014/07/31/banking-for-the-poor-will-this-be-bill-gatess-greatest-philanthropic-achievement/.
13. Andrew Cave, “Banking for the Poor: Will This Be Bill Gates’ Greatest Philanthropic Achievement?,” *Forbes Online*, July 31, 2014, accessed October 1, 2014, http://www.forbes.com/sites/andrewcave/2014/07/31/banking-for-the-poor-will-this-be-bill-gatess-greatest-philanthropic-achievement/.
14. Andrew Cave, “Banking for the Poor: Will This Be Bill Gates’ Greatest Philanthropic Achievement?,” *Forbes Online*, July 31, 2014, accessed October 1, 2014, http://www.forbes.com/sites/andrewcave/2014/07/31/banking-for-the-poor-will-this-be-bill-gatess-greatest-philanthropic-achievement/.
15. Andrew Cave, “Banking for the Poor: Will This Be Bill Gates’ Greatest Philanthropic Achievement?,” *Forbes Online*, July 31, 2014, accessed October 1, 2014, http://www.forbes.com/sites/andrewcave/2014/07/31/banking-for-the-poor-will-this-be-bill-gatess-greatest-philanthropic-achievement/.
16. “Who Are the Unbanked?,” Citi FT Financial Education Summit 2014 site, accessed October 1, 2014, http://event.ft-live.com/ehome/finedu2014/unbankedInfographic/?&.
17. Heidi Garrett-Peltier, James Heintz, and Robert Pollin, *How Infrastructure Investments Support the U.S. Economy: Employment,*

*Productivity and Growth,* Political Economy Research Institute, University of Massachusetts Amherst, January 2009, accessed October 1, 2014, http://www.peri.umass.edu/fileadmin/pdf/other_publication_types/green_economics/PERI_Infrastructure_Investments.

18. *Is It Time for an Infrastructure Push? The Macroeconomic Effects of Public Investment,* International Monetary Fund, accessed October 1, 2014, http://www.imf.org/external/pubs/ft/weo/2014/02/pdf/c3.pdf.
19. *Is It Time for an Infrastructure Push? The Macroeconomic Effects of Public Investment,* International Monetary Fund, accessed October 1, 2014, http://www.imf.org/external/pubs/ft/weo/2014/02/pdf/c3.pdf.
20. *Infrastructure Investment Policy Blueprint,* World Economic Forum, February 2014, accessed October 1, 2014, http://www.weforum.org/reports/infrastructure-investment-policy-blueprint.
21. *Infrastructure Investment Policy Blueprint,* World Economic Forum, February 2014, accessed October 1, 2014, http://www.weforum.org/reports/infrastructure-investment-policy-blueprint.
22. *Infrastructure Investment Policy Blueprint,* World Economic Forum, February 2014, accessed October 1, 2014, http://www.weforum.org/reports/infrastructure-investment-policy-blueprint.
23. *Infrastructure Investment Policy Blueprint,* World Economic Forum, February 2014, accessed October 1, 2014, http://www.weforum.org/reports/infrastructure-investment-policy-blueprint.
24. "Reducing Airport Delays: Reconstruction of the Bay Runway at John F. Kennedy International Airport," Port Authority of New York and New Jersey, accessed October 1, 2014, http://www.panynj.gov/airports/pdf/jfk-runway-project.pdf.
25. "Reducing Airport Delays: Reconstruction of the Bay Runway at John F. Kennedy International Airport," Port Authority of New York and New Jersey, accessed October 1, 2014, http://www.panynj.gov/airports/pdf/jfk-runway-project.pdf.
26. "TheVictorianDesalinationProject,"Aquasure,accessedOctober1,2014, http://www.aquasure.com.au/desalination-plant.
27. "The Victorian Desalination Project," Aquasure, accessed October 1, 2014, http://www.aquasure.com.au/desalination-plant.
28. "The Victorian Desalination Project," Aquasure, accessed October 1, 2014, http://www.aquasure.com.au/desalination-plant.
29. "Bujagali Energy Successfully Delivering First 50mw of Clean Energy to the Ugandan Electricity Grid" (press release), Blackstone, March 19, 2012, accessed October 1, 2014, http://www

.blackstone.com/news-views/press-releases/details/bujagali-energy-sucessfully-delivering-first-50mw-of-clean-energy-to-the-ugandan-electricity-grid.

30. "Bujagali Energy Successfully Delivering First 50mw of Clean Energy to the Ugandan Electricity Grid" (press release), Blackstone, March 19, 2012, accessed October 1, 2014, http://www.blackstone.com/news-views/press-releases/details/bujagali-energy-sucessfully-delivering-first-50mw-of-clean-energy-to-the-ugandan-electricity-grid.
31. "Bujagali Energy Successfully Delivering First 50mw of Clean Energy to the Ugandan Electricity Grid" (press release), Blackstone, March 19, 2012, accessed October 1, 2014, http://www.blackstone.com/news-views/press-releases/details/bujagali-energy-sucessfully-delivering-first-50mw-of-clean-energy-to-the-ugandan-electricity-grid.
32. "Bujagali Energy Successfully Delivering First 50mw of Clean Energy to the Ugandan Electricity Grid" (press release), Blackstone, March 19, 2012, accessed October 1, 2014, http://www.blackstone.com/news-views/press-releases/details/bujagali-energy-sucessfully-delivering-first-50mw-of-clean-energy-to-the-ugandan-electricity-grid.
33. "Successful Rehabilitation Will Deliver Real Benefits to Society," Social Finance Ltd., accessed October 1, 2014, http://www.socialfinance.org.uk/impact/criminal-justice/.
34. Susannah Birkwood, "Peterborough Prison Social Impact Bond Pilot Fails to Hit Target to Trigger Repayments," *Third Sector*, August 7, 2014, accessed October 1, 2014, http://www.thirdsector.co.uk/peterborough-prison-social-impact-bond-pilot-fails-hit-target-trigger-repayments/finance/article/1307031.
35. Susannah Birkwood, "Peterborough Prison Social Impact Bond Pilot Fails to Hit Target to Trigger Repayments," *Third Sector*, August 7, 2014, accessed October 1, 2014, http://www.thirdsector.co.uk/peterborough-prison-social-impact-bond-pilot-fails-hit-target-trigger-repayments/finance/article/1307031.
36. Susannah Birkwood, "Peterborough Prison Social Impact Bond Pilot Fails to Hit Target to Trigger Repayments," *Third Sector*, August 7, 2014, accessed October 1, 2014, http://www.thirdsector.co.uk/peterborough-prison-social-impact-bond-pilot-fails-hit-target-trigger-repayments/finance/article/1307031.
37. Susannah Birkwood, "Peterborough Prison Social Impact Bond Pilot Fails to Hit Target to Trigger Repayments," *Third Sector*, August 7, 2014, accessed October 1, 2014, http://www.thirdsector.co.uk/peterborough

-prison-social-impact-bond-pilot-fails-hit-target-trigger-repayments/finance/article/1307031.

38. "Social Impact Bond for Early Childhood Education," Goldman Sachs Urban Investments, accessed October 1, 2014, http://www.goldmansachs.com/what-we-do/investing-and-lending/urban-investments/case-studies/salt-lake-social-impact-bond.html.
39. "Social Impact Bond for Early Childhood Education," Goldman Sachs Urban Investments, accessed October 1, 2014, http://www.goldmansachs.com/what-we-do/investing-and-lending/urban-investments/case-studies/salt-lake-social-impact-bond.html.
40. "Social Impact Bond for Early Childhood Education," Goldman Sachs Urban Investments, accessed October 1, 2014, http://www.goldmansachs.com/what-we-do/investing-and-lending/urban-investments/case-studies/salt-lake-social-impact-bond.html.
41. "Charitable Giving Statistics," National Philanthropic Trust, accessed October 1, 2014, http://www.nptrust.org/philanthropic-resources/charitable-giving-statistics/.
42. *The 2014 U.S. Trust Study of High Net Worth Philanthropy,* Bank of America, accessed October 1, 2014, http://newsroom.bankofamerica.com/sites/bankofamerica.newshq.businesswire.com/files/press_kit/additional/2014_US_Trust_Study_of_High_Net_Worth_Philanthropy.pdf.
43. *The 2014 U.S. Trust Study of High Net Worth Philanthropy,* Bank of America, accessed October 1, 2014, http://newsroom.bankofamerica.com/sites/bankofamerica.newshq.businesswire.com/files/press_kit/additional/2014_US_Trust_Study_of_High_Net_Worth_Philanthropy.pdf.
44. *The 2014 U.S. Trust Study of High Net Worth Philanthropy,* Bank of America, accessed October 1, 2014, http://newsroom.bankofamerica.com/sites/bankofamerica.newshq.businesswire.com/files/press_kit/additional/2014_US_Trust_Study_of_High_Net_Worth_Philanthropy.pdf.
45. *The 2014 U.S. Trust Study of High Net Worth Philanthropy,* Bank of America, accessed October 1, 2014, http://newsroom.bankofamerica.com/sites/bankofamerica.newshq.businesswire.com/files/press_kit/additional/2014_US_Trust_Study_of_High_Net_Worth_Philanthropy.pdf.
46. *The 2014 U.S. Trust Study of High Net Worth Philanthropy,* Bank of America, accessed October 1, 2014, http://newsroom.bankofamerica

.com/sites/bankofamerica.newshq.businesswire.com/files/press_kit/additional/2014_US_Trust_Study_of_High_Net_Worth_Philanthropy.pdf.

47. *The 2014 U.S. Trust Study of High Net Worth Philanthropy,* Bank of America, accessed October 1, 2014, http://newsroom.bankofamerica.com/sites/bankofamerica.newshq.businesswire.com/files/press_kit/additional/2014_US_Trust_Study_of_High_Net_Worth_Philanthropy.pdf.
48. *The 2014 U.S. Trust Study of High Net Worth Philanthropy,* Bank of America, accessed October 1, 2014, http://newsroom.bankofamerica.com/sites/bankofamerica.newshq.businesswire.com/files/press_kit/additional/2014_US_Trust_Study_of_High_Net_Worth_Philanthropy.pdf.
49. *The 2014 U.S. Trust Study of High Net Worth Philanthropy,* Bank of America, accessed October 1, 2014, http://newsroom.bankofamerica.com/sites/bankofamerica.newshq.businesswire.com/files/press_kit/additional/2014_US_Trust_Study_of_High_Net_Worth_Philanthropy.pdf.
50. "Frequently Asked Questions," The National Center for Charitable Statistics, accessed October 1, 2014, http://foundationcenter.org/getstarted/faqs/html/howmany.html.
51. *The 2014 U.S. Trust Study of High Net Worth Philanthropy,* Bank of America, accessed October 1, 2014, http://newsroom.bankofamerica.com/sites/bankofamerica.newshq.businesswire.com/files/press_kit/additional/2014_US_Trust_Study_of_High_Net_Worth_Philanthropy.pdf.
52. *The 2014 U.S. Trust Study of High Net Worth Philanthropy,* Bank of America, accessed October 1, 2014, http://newsroom.bankofamerica.com/sites/bankofamerica.newshq.businesswire.com/files/press_kit/additional/2014_US_Trust_Study_of_High_Net_Worth_Philanthropy.pdf.
53. *Global Pension Assets Study 2014,* Towers Watson, January 2014, accessed October 1, 2014, http://conferences.pionline.com/assets/2014_GPAS_Study_Final.pdf.
54. "Reports," Activist Insight, accessed October 1, 2014, http://www.activistinsight.com/Reports.aspx.
55. "CDP 2013 Sector Insights," PwC, accessed October 1, 2014, http://www.pwc.com/gx/en/sustainability/publications/carbon-disclosure-project/index.jhtml.

## Conclusion

1. "Emerging and Developing Economies Much More Optimistic than Rich Countries about the Future," Pew Research Center, accessed October 9, 2014, http://www.pewglobal.org/2014/10/09/emerging-and-developing-economies-much-more-optimistic-than-rich-countries-about-the-future/.
2. "For Most Workers, Real Wages Have Barely Budged for Decades," *FactTank* (blog), Pew Research Center, accessed October 9, 2014, http://www.pewresearch.org/fact-tank/2014/10/09/for-most-workers-real-wages-have-barely-budged-for-decades/.
3. "For Most Workers, Real Wages Have Barely Budged for Decades," *FactTank* (blog), Pew Research Center, accessed October 9, 2014, http://www.pewresearch.org/fact-tank/2014/10/09/for-most-workers-real-wages-have-barely-budged-for-decades/.
4. Matthew Boesler, "Greenspan Sees Turmoil as QE Boost to Markets Unwinds," *Bloomberg,* October 30, 2014, accessed October 30, 2014, http://www.bloomberg.com/news/2014-10-29/greenspan-sees-turmoil-as-qe-boost-to-markets-unwinds.html.
5. *Global Wealth Report 2014,* Credit Suisse, accessed October 1, 2014, https://publications.credit-suisse.com/tasks/render/file/?fileID=60931FDE-A2D2-F568-B041B58C5EA591A4.
6. "Working for the Few," OXFAM, accessed October 1, 2014, http://www.oxfam.org/sites/www.oxfam.org/files/bp-working-for-few-political-capture-economic-inequality-200114-summ-en.pdf.
7. Shawn Donnan, "UK Study in Call to Unleash $1tn for Social Investments," *Financial Times,* September 14, 2014, accessed October 1, 2014, http://www.ft.com/cms/s/0/bbcd03f6-3a89-11e4-bd08-00144feabdc0.html#ixzz3DKbqBJxG.
8. *From the Margins to the Mainstream,* World Economic Forum, September 2013, accessed October 1, 2014, http://www3.weforum.org/docs/WEF_II_FromMarginsMainstream_Report_2013.pdf.
9. Shawn Donnan, "UK Study in Call to Unleash $1tn for Social Investments," *Financial Times,* September 14, 2014, accessed October 1, 2014, http://www.ft.com/cms/s/0/bbcd03f6-3a89-11e4-bd08-00144feabdc0.html#ixzz3DKbqBJxG.
10. "Monthly Report," World Federation of Exchanges, accessed October 1, 2014, http://www.world-exchanges.org/statistics/monthly-reports.

11. *Global Pension Assets Study 2014,* Towers Watson, January 2014, accessed October 1, 2014, http://conferences.pionline.com/assets/2014_GPAS_Study_Final.pdf.
12. "World Population Projected to Reach 9.6 Billion by 2050," United Nations Department of Economic and Social Affairs, accessed October 1, 2014, https://www.un.org/en/development/desa/news/population/un-report-world-population-projected-to-reach-9-6-billion-by-2050.html.
13. David Madland and Ruy Teixeira, "New Progressive America: The Millennial Generation," Center for American Progress, May 13, 2009, accessed October 1, 2014, http://www.americanprogress.org/issues/progressive-movement/report/2009/05/13/6133/new-progressive-america-the-millennial-generation/.
14. Jeanne Meister, "Three Reasons You Need to Adopt a Millennial Mindset Regardless of Your Age," *Forbes Online,* October 5, 2012, accessed October 1, 2014, http://www.forbes.com/sites/jeannemeister/2012/10/05/millennialmindse/.
15. *The Millennial Survey 2014,* Deloitte, accessed October 1, 2014, http://www2.deloitte.com/global/en/pages/about-deloitte/articles/2014-millennial-survey-positive-impact.html.
16. *From the Margins to the Mainstream,* World Economic Forum, September 2013, accessed October 1, 2014, http://www3.weforum.org/docs/WEF_II_FromMarginsMainstream_Report_2013.pdf.

# Index

# Index

# Index

## Index

Index

# Index

# Index

# Index

# About the Author

Jeremy K. Balkin is regarded as an international expert on ethics in banking, impact investing, and the strategic engagement of millennials in financial services. In 2008, he survived a life-changing extreme sports injury that shaped his purpose to deploy financial resources to improve the state of the world.

The *Huffington Post* described Jeremy K. Balkin as the "Anti-Wolf of Wall Street" for his work making the case that banking and finance are forces for good. His popular TEDx talk, "The Noble Cause: Positively Influencing the Allocation of Capital" has been viewed over a quarter million times, and he has been invited to speak at Davos, the United Nations, and London School of Economics.

Jeremy K. Balkin has run five marathons, received the prestigious UNSW Alumni Award for Achievement, and is designated as a Young Global Leader by the World Economic Forum. He has studied at the UNSW Business School, Financial Services Institute of Australasia, and Harvard Kennedy School.